The Strugglers

RETHINKING READING

Series Editor: L. John Chapman,
School of Education, The Open University

Current titles:

L. John Chapman   *Reading: From 5–11 years*

Christine Davis and   *Shared Reading in Practice*
Rosemary Stubbs

Tony Martin   *The Strugglers: Working with children who fail to learn to read*

The Strugglers

Working with children who fail to learn to read

TONY MARTIN

Open University Press
Milton Keynes · Philadelphia

Open University Press
12 Cofferidge Close
Stony Stratford
Milton Keynes MK11 1BY, England

and

242 Cherry Street
Philadelphia, PA 19106, USA

First Published 1989

British Library Cataloguing in Publication Data

Martin, Tony
    The strugglers: working with children
who fail to learn to read.—(Rethinking
reading).
1. Reading disordered children. Remedial
education
I. Title II. Series
371.91′4

ISBN 0-335-09512-7
ISBN 0-335-09511-9 Pbk

Typeset by Burns and Smith, Derby
Printed in Great Britain by St Edmundsbury Press, Bury St Edmunds

To Lance, Karl, Gasparro, Stephen,
Herbie and Jennifer
The group who made me think.

Contents

Introduction		1
1.	Leslie: a reading failure talks about failing	5
2.	The de-skilling of teachers	18
3.	Early stages: Jenny, 4 years old, demonstrates the process	28
4.	How Sally solved the mystery of *Tom's Midnight Garden*	38
5.	Organizing a programme	46
6.	Readers and books: literature for the failures	57
Appendix		82
Bibliography		85
Index		86

Introduction

Bog off! I ain't reading that babby stuff!

(Jennifer, a non-reader, aged nine)

In order to explain how I came to write this book I ought to begin with some history. In September 1980 I was deputy head of a middle school in Worcestershire, where I had been developing the language curriculum for a number of years. While I felt that much of the work was heading in the right direction and indeed in some areas was very exciting, one aspect remained distinctly unsatisfactory. Each year a number of children would arrive from the first schools with problems with their reading and writing and then leave us four years later still suffering from the same problems. I am not suggesting that no progress was made or that they were neglected, but the fact remained that on arrival at the high school they were usually still unable to function as independent and fluent readers and writers. They had been identified in the first schools early on in their school careers as having problems and it appeared that the chances were that they would leave school to become adults with the same problems. I wondered whether there was anything we could do about it. I decided that I would try and set up some sort of a system to provide help.

Despite the fact that my subject specialism was language I was the first to admit that I knew little about working with children who had reading and writing difficulties. That was the province of the special needs teams (the remedial lady as she was called) and the educational pyschologists: specialists who possessed mysterious expertise centred around tests for scientific- and medical-sounding disabilities. If I was going to work with such children then I must first learn about how to do so. Therefore during that summer holiday I acquired as many books on the subject as I could lay my hands on. I read avidly and I made equipment. I made work cards, flash cards, games and posters, all centred around words and what they looked and sounded like. This was the message that came through very strongly from the books I read. The children I was going to help had failed with ordinary teaching and would respond better to an approach which was active and enjoyable and different.

Armed with my teaching aids and a pile of The Neale Analysis of Reading I arrived back at school in September feeling very excited. I had decided to operate a system of withdrawal each day of a small group of children with the worst problems. I had the first school records and had met the teachers to discuss the children concerned, so all that remained was to test the children with Neale to determine the nature of their particular problems. Then I could provide each child with work aimed at these problems. Some would require help with phonics, others with comprehension, perhaps a few with initial digraphs. And in fact that is exactly what happened (apart from the two who could not read anything on the Neale, but I had my flash cards of sounds for them). The children would arrive each day in my room and get on with their own particular course of work while I heard individuals read from the sets of books written especially for remedial readers (Shorty, Monster, Bangers and Mash, Whizz Bang etc). Regularly we would work together, playing games or trying to read the posters which adorned the room: P-m h-d a fl-n in the p-n . . . J-ck put a cl-ck in his s-ck . . . The games were very popular, especially Hunt and Stab which involved spreading cards on which were written words all over a table. The children stood around a table with their hands behind their backs and I would call out a word. The first child to 'stab' the word with his finger was able to keep it. At the end of the game the child with the most words was declared the winner.

And so the year passed with the children making variable progress. One boy became a fluent reader by Christmas (just ten weeks of remedial help), two others were well on their way by July. Most had made some progress when I re-tested them on the Neale at the end of the year. One appeared beyond help! I suppose if I had been asked what I expected at the outset my reply would have been much as it turned out. So I should have felt satisfied. I suppose in some respects I did feel pleased, especially when talking on parents evening to two mothers of children in the group. They were so delighted by the progress their children had made, admitting to having despaired of this ever happening. I was very moved by what they said. Yet as I packed things away for the summer holiday the year kept nagging at me. Was I really sure what had happened? I had this strange feeling of dissatisfaction with what had gone on. But it would not crystallize into words. At different times as I looked towards the next year it returned until at last I realized what it was. For three school terms I had taught the group and the children had progressed at different rates. But there did not seem to be any connection between my teaching and the children's progress. Had Ambrose really learned to read in one term because of the comprehension work cards and the Monster books? Why had the others not made really dramatic progress over the year with all the time they had spent working on my materials? What exactly was the connection between my teaching and their learning? I had this sneaking suspicion that progress had been made despite the games and cards, while phonic flash cards did not appear to have much to do with becoming a fluent reader.

However, as I prepared for the new school year I had no alternative but to persevere with the same strategies. I did not know what else to try. Further reading of books concerned with reading problems confirmed that what I had been doing was correct. So I continued for another year. It was at this point that I was fortunate to be given a year's secondment to Birmingham University to do a course in language. As it turned out there was little on this course to do with 'remedial' children but during the year I read Frank Smith's *Reading* new edn. (1986). And what a bombshell that was! Here were all of the nagging doubts about what I had been doing. Here was a view of reading which just made so much sense, and seemed to have so many implications for the children I had been working with. Soon after, Margaret Meek's *Achieving Literacy* (1983) was published and again I found myself fascinated and excited by what I read. No answers here but lots of questions, and a message that altered my thinking about this whole area: we must see the difficulty from the child's viewpoint. In addition Margaret Meek's book gave me tremendous confidence through her insistence that nobody really knows how most children learn to read fluently, and why some fail to do so is even more of a mystery. I realized that I need not be dependent on the ideas contained in all of those books about children with reading problems, especially when they had made me feel so uneasy. I could explore the problems my children had (with them) and see if the sorts of strategies suggested by *Reading* and *Achieving Literacy* had anything to offer. I had a gut feeling that they had.

Over the next three years I worked very closely with a group of children (all aged nine when we started) and the ideas developed as we went along. Many of the things we tried were abandoned while others appeared to offer hope of real progress, but an underlying rationale slowly emerged upon which our work eventually became based. It is this rationale which lies at the heart of this book.

From the beginning there was a growing belief that while the children I was working with most certainly did have 'special needs' it did not necessarily follow that they required a 'special' curriculum. The more we worked together the further away we got from the ideas contained in the books and articles I had read initially. Where we ended up is contained in later chapters, but none of this work appeared in books written for teachers working with children who had reading and writing difficulties. In the case of reading I have a great interest in the world of children's literature and was becoming fascinated by the implications of the theories of the reader-response critics to children as readers (as a result of my year at Birmingham). There were so many connections with the ideas of Frank Smith and others writing about reading. All of this seemed particularly relevant to the children I knew who were struggling to read. Yet the world of literature was scarcely mentioned in the 'remedial' books; certainly a chapter concerned with developing response to fiction or poetry would have seemed totally out of place. I became convinced that the way readers respond to literature is of great relevance to all children and has enormous implications for all primary teachers. Children who are struggling need this sort of work most of all. The hope is that through this book teachers whose major interest and role within education is 'special needs' will be made aware of the exciting work now going on in the field of children's literature: work which they may well miss because the books in which it appears do not seem to be of direct relevance to them. In addition I believe it provides approaches to reading in mixed-ability classrooms which will enable primary-class teachers to work effectively with all children, whether they have reading problems or not.

The second strategy which became a major aspect of my work has already been mentioned, and is dramatically illustrated in the first chapter. This is a deeply held belief that we, as teachers, should always attempt to see things from the child's viewpoint. All too often we become so tied up in our teaching that we lose touch with the children's learning. We know what we are doing, why we have decided on certain teaching strategies and the progression the work will take. But how does the child view all of this? Are his perceptions of why he is being asked to work in a particular way the same as ours? Chapter 1 shows how 10- and 11-year-old 'reading failures' are most certainly thinking about their predicament, searching for clues to success. Sometimes what they perceive to be important is not what we intended. Perhaps then it does not lead to improvement. When this happens over and over again, they despair, either passively accepting what we give them or rebelling against the whole situation. We need to discover what the children think.

Finally the two other strategies were connected in that they were ways of providing the maximum support for the children. They needed to learn to read with their parents if at all possible and they needed a method which removed as far as possible the stress and strain they felt when they read. Parents were then involved in helping at home on what could be called a shared reading programme, reading with their child rather than hearing them read. Over three years the amount of reading at home varied tremendously but those children who had the most support were the ones who made the most progress.

What follows is an attempt to consider the areas outlined above. It reflects work which slowly evolved over a number of years and offers a chance to stand back and consider what we do, suggesting that perhaps certain ways of working have more to offer than what goes on at present in many classrooms. The main reason why I became so convinced of the rightness of this work was that it was ultimately based on what children were telling me about their reading. I worked closely with three fluent 9-year-olds as they read novels, and explored what they seemed to be doing and what seemed to be important to them. I tried to build up close enough relationships with the 'strugglers' so that they felt secure enough to try and discuss their problems and how they were trying to cope with them. It is on the basis of the words of these children, quoted at some length in the following chapters, that my ideas grew.

CHAPTER 1

Leslie: a reading failure talks about failing

. . . our pupils' views of what learning to read means may have very little in common with our own.

(Margaret Meek 1983)

We must begin with the child. For too long we have neglected the thoughts and feelings of the child failing to make progress in reading. We have concentrated on determining what such a child cannot do and have then tried to devise approaches which will bring about improvement. We have known the reasons for the programmes of work but have we made these reasons known to the child? Have we asked him why he cannot read? Have we asked him for his views on the nature of reading? I believe that at the centre of working with reading failures should be a relationship between pupil and teacher which takes into account and tries to explore the former's feelings and perceptions about the situation.

In September 1982 a 9-year-old boy, I will call him Leslie, arrived at a middle school. He was unable to read. Nearly three years later he was on the verge of becoming an independent reader. He could manage the most difficult 'graded' books and many of the 'ordinary' paperbacks (he had read Roald Dahl's *The Magic Finger* and Joan Aiken's *A Necklace of Raindrops* among others). He was attempting to bridge the gulf which separated him from other novels aimed at his age group and was reading Gene Kemp's *The Turbulent Term of Tyke Tyler* with me. He was managing – with help.

In three years Leslie had changed from a boy who cried in lessons, 'couldn't do' any of the tasks asked of him, had nightmares about school (according to his mother) and had been diagnosed by a psychologist as 'worthy' of a place at a special school to a lively, cheerful 12-year-old who sang in the school choir, put a tremendous amount of effort into his school work and contributed well to life in the classroom.

The purpose of this chapter is not to chart Leslie's progress but to illustrate two fundamental points. Firstly it is to try and indicate what was actually going on in the mind of a reading 'failure' as he failed. Leslie had proved to be a very articulate boy and agreed to talk on tape about what he remembered of his time at first school as he failed to learn to read. Most of the chapter is a transcript of that tape. While it is to be hoped that teachers have reasons for doing what they do when they 'teach' reading, we should remember that young children will also develop a view of the tasks they have to undertake. Most, of course, learn to read so quickly and automatically that they have little time to ponder and worry, but the failure must surely wonder why.

Secondly the comments of teachers taken from Leslie's record cards are given as an indication of the 'official' position. These are permanent statements which remain with Leslie for years. However, when set against the real Leslie, thinking and feeling about what happened to himself at school they are shown to be (as are most such records?) somewhat inadequate and even misleading.

Firstly we read the summaries of Leslie's teachers. Under the heading 'Language' on his first-school record cards is written:

September 1978 C.A. 5 + .
Leslie enjoys participating in class discussions. He copies under the teacher's writing and has made slow progress with reading probably due to lack of concentration.

September 1979 C.A. 6 + .
Leslie enjoys talking. He has begun to write a sentence or two of his own, but with difficulty. We had to go back to the beginning of the reading scheme earlier this year as Leslie had forgotten previous work. He is now doing quite well with Ladybird 3b.

September 1980 C.A. 7 + .
Ladybird 3b. Free writing is almost absent, 'Read, Write and Remember' comprehension 2. Poor spelling – tries to be tidy. Contributes warmly to class talks.

September 1981 C.A. 8 + .
Leslie is still 'struggling' with reading. He has finished 5a with a great deal of help and has been transferred to Griffin Pirates to see if he can achieve a little more success with these. He is very neat and can write a page of free writing but this is lacking in interest.
[Leslie actually spent the last two years in the same class with the same teacher. He had been considered too poor to manage in the top class.]

I do not intend commenting upon these statements. The layout of most record cards demands brevity on the part of teachers and I will do no more here than question their value. The transcript which follows displays how little they tell us about Leslie, his problems and how best he could be helped.

Question   Can you remember what your first day at school was like?
Leslie   Horrible – I was really scared – and the teacher asked me a question and I couldn't answer it and another kid put up his hand and he could and it made me go all funny – inside – and I was thinking 'oh I couldn't do that and he could'.

Q What do you remember about reading?

L They kept giving you books over – like when you went onto a book, right, and then you finish it and then you go onto another one the teacher would say if you can't read that one go back onto the other one – well I've read it again, so that's a bit boring – she never gave, you know, a different book, a smaller one but a different story – she's just giving you the same books.

Q The same books over and over?

L Yeah, till you got it right.

Q How long did it take you sometimes to get it right?

L Half a term! [laughs] Yeah because some of the words are hard – see – she never gave me no easy ones. Like the pirate, the blue pirate and the red pirate, books like that – that's how it was really scary.

Q Why was it really scary?

L Well the teacher – and you come into school [laughs] ...

Q But the pirate books are quite hard. What were you reading before them?

L I weren't reading anything – just words – on cards – only letters and words – she used to put them up and you had to say it – and you had to say your alphabet and that.

Q So you can remember what the first book was you ever had?

L [Pause] Peter and Jane. That was the first one I ever had. Peter and Jane and then I went on to the pirate ones.

Q How many Peter and Jane books did you read?

L [Pause] Twenty? About twenty. And this kid right, some kids had thick books and there's me with the book this thin [laughs] – really shy and everything – it's funny – and then I started to pick up and then I lost it again.

Q What happened?

L I stopped reading – like you say 'don't stop reading' – well I stopped reading.

Q Why?

L Because I liked, I liked, I'd rather do drawing – because I do that lots at home – and I stopped reading.

Q So you stopped reading at school and you just did drawing at school?

L Not just – we did have to do a bit of reading.

Q To yourself, to another child, to the teacher?

L To the teacher most of the time – never by yourself – they never let you have a chance – they think, oh no, let's listen to him.

Q Why didn't you ever read on your own do you think? Did the other children read on their own?.

L Yeah – and they just – and my brother has to read to the teacher as well – he has trouble with reading.

Q So the ones who weren't very good read to the teacher a lot?

L Yeah.

Q Did you ever read on your own?

L I did at home. We took the books home.

Q   Did you read to your mum?

L   Teacher said read a page on your own, right, and read it over again to your mum.

Q   So why did you stop reading?

L   It was boring reading just reading the same books.

Q   How good were you then?

L   Medium.

Q   So there were children worse than you?.

L   Yeah – a few – a bit worse – that's what made me happy.

Q   But you came up here about *the* worst. So what went wrong?

L   *The worst*?!

Q   Well who was worse than you?

L   [Pause] Well, I'll tell you what happened. I was in this class, right, and I was moving up to the top class but they kept me in the same class. So I was in with the young ones. I was in that one class. I wasn't brainy enough to go up to the other classes.

Q   But you said you were in the middle so why didn't they put you up?

L   I dunno. That's what made me think. It was just the same – with the books and everything – I was two years in that class.

Q   And did the teacher do different work with you?

L   Yes – different work.

Q   And how did you do?

L   I did all right but then I just dropped down.

Q   Why?

L   [Pause] I can't think . . . Why did I drop down? Cos I didn't try.

Q   Why not?

L   Cos I didn't think I'd learn.

Q   What do you mean?

L   Well, I could read, but I wouldn't be able to do writing and spelling and that – so I just dropped down.

Q   So your reading was good enough for you to say you could read?

L   Well I was bad but they were easy books. They were easier.

Q   Were there children in your class reading harder books then?

L   Yeah – pretty hard – they used to have library books and I used to have them little books from outside and I used to go out and pick them.

Q   Was that good, going out to get your books?

L   Yeah – cos some like me used to be out there as well, see, I can't remember their names and they just picked up. And there's me [laughs] – there'd be green and blue and red and I was always on orange . . . that's me.

Q   So you'd sit down to read and you'd come to a word you couldn't read. Why couldn't you read it?

L   [Pause] That's a difficult thing!

Q I know!

L Why couldn't I read the word? I couldn't – I wouldn't – well, you know the alphabet, say u or v – I wouldn't really know what those letters are – so I couldn't read it.

Q But what about the teacher holding up the letter cards?

L Cos all the class used to say it. And I used to join in with that – if they'd start to say 'cu' I'd say 'cu' really quickly [laughs].

Q So she didn't do this work just with you ever?

L No. Well there was sometimes three or two of us – and they'd say 'cu' and I'd say 'cu' [laughs].

Q So you knew you didn't know it. Why didn't you tell the teacher?

L She'd tell me off. I was scared – cos I didn't know the word.

Q So you thought that if you knew your letters of the alphabet you'd be able to read?

L Yeah. That's what I kept doing – trying on the letters – oh, if I could get this alphabet I could read all the words. But I didn't – I couldn't read all the words.

Q Even when you knew the alphabet?

L Yeah.

Q Why not?

L Well, you know like 'ch' – you see, then I couldn't put them together – like 'eat' or 'home'. I couldn't put the letters together to make that word. So even when I learnt the alphabet I couldn't do it. Funny ain't it really [laughs].

Q So what did you do then? Is that when you gave up or did you do something else?

L [Pause] I did something else. Learn the words. You know, if I was stuck on a word, teacher used to give us a book and we'd write it and take it home to learn.

Q Learn that one word?

L Yeah.

Q Did she give you any words like it? A pattern – cat, bat, sat?

L Just that one word.

Q So you had long lists of words to take home?

L Yes.

Q Did you find you could recognize them when they came up in the book?

L Sometimes . . . Sometimes not.

Q Why did you think you were learning to read?

L Cos everybody else was. And when you grew up it would help you to get a good job. So I could get a good job.

Q Did you like books?

L Yeah.

Q Even though you found it difficult?

L Yeah.

Q Did you used to worry about your reading getting nowhere?

L Yeah. If I went to visit a place – and someone might say 'read that to me' and you'd be scared and have to say 'I can't read it' [laughs].

Q Why couldn't you read it?

L . . . it was smaller and I thought that's really hard cos they're smaller – and I thought I can't read that cos they're smaller – it made me think after a bit – they used to give us books with big words in and then the teacher gave me a book with smaller words in and I thought that was harder. Like in the newspapers – really small [laughs]. And the teacher gave it to me and I took it home and I couldn't read it – so my mum read it to me – so I took it back to the school and told the teacher I couldn't read it and she heard me a bit and said I'd better go back to the little books – Peter and Jane [laughs].

Q Were they exciting books Peter and Jane?

L No – they like went to the park! But there was this brilliant one which I read over and over again – when they went to the seaside.

Q And could you read that?

L No! My mum told me some words and then I looked at the pictures – and then I got to know it and could read it over and over again . . . that's another thing – if a book didn't have pictures in I'd think, oh that's hard cos it's got no pictures in – it's all writing – no pictures to help me – cos that's how I used to do it – I used to look at the pictures first and then the word – always the picture first cos I thought it would help me – sometimes it did but sometimes it didn't – like if in the picture they're playing I'd see a word beginning with 'p' and I'd say playing.

Q What if you were wrong?

L Then the teacher would tell me to write it in my book and take it home to learn.

Q Tell me about reading to the headmistress.

L Well I used to read to the headmistress.

Q Well, what happened?

L Well I was scared cos it was the headmistress. So I tried as hard as I could and not get a word wrong cos it made me all embarrassed.

Q So what happened. You'd go in with your book and stand next to her and what happened?

L Reading! I'd start reading and I'd get slower and slower and I usually get stuck on a word – and that's what made me embarrassed.

Q And then?

L She'd usually go like this – like the word – she'd go 'what's that?' and I'd go 'ch'.

Q She'd split the word up?

L Yeah. And I didn't know what it was and then she'd go, 'it's 'cl', Leslie, 'cl'. And I'd go, 'cl . . . classroom!' [laughs].

Q So you had four years over there with all of the teachers helping you and the headmistress and yet you gave up. I've known you for two and a half years and you're reading. How come you couldn't do it over there?

L It was boring. They kept giving you the same books over and over again. That's why. I just gave up. If they couldn't give me proper books to read.

Q Was that the main thing?

L Oh no. That'd be my words. You know – to get it really right – and she'd say, 'what does that mean?' And she'd say the word – I didn't know what it meant.

Q What, words you never heard of before in the books?

L Yeah – and if you never knew the meaning you couldn't get the story could you – so it'd be really boring, the story, if you didn't know what it meant.

Q What about now? When we're reading, say Dr Dolittle, are there lots of words you don't know?

L Yes and no. Some I know, some I don't.

Q What sort of writing did you do at school in your first class?

L [Pause] Copy off the board. Cos she writ everything on the board and what we had to do was copy it off – I reckon that was the problem – if I was a teacher I would've said 'write a story' – she just writ everything on the board and we had to copy. Just copy.

Q What sort of things did she write on the board?

L Can't really remember [pause] – oh, a story. And we had to copy it.

Q Was that the first class?

L No.

Q What about the first class?

L We had sentences without an ending and you had to write the ending.

Q What about your own writing? Stories? News? Making up your own things?

L Yeah – a little book – a story book.

Q Were your stories any good? Did *you* think they were?

L I thought they was. I don't know about the teacher [laughs]!

Q Why not? Didn't she tell you?

L No – she used to put a tick and one of them stars – and she used to put 'good' – but she never used to tell me if it was really good, you know, very good.

Q What was your handwriting like then?

L Don't say!

Q Why not?

L Awful [laughs]!

Q Why?

L My hs would be upside down and everything – all the wrong way round.

Q Why?

L Why? Why? I dunno why? There must be an answer!

Q I wonder why you wrote hs upside down?

L [Pause] Oh yeah – I always thought an h was a u – that's why – cos a u looks like an h – when they used to say, 'draw one of those, with a stick up', I used to do one and it looks like an h upside down. You get me?

Q   Yes I do. Does that mean that the writing could still be as good even with the letters upside down?

L   Yes. Cos I would say, 'that's supposed to be an h'.

Q   Could the teacher have read it without your help?

L   No! Obble Obble Obble Obble Obble – Chinese [laughs]!

Q   But could *you* read it?

L   Yeah – cos I writ the story.

Q   When you first came here you used to sit and burst into tears when I used to ask you to do any work.

L   I didn't!

Q   The first lesson you came to me you burst into tears and you sat with your head in your arms and you wouldn't do any work.

L   I didn't.

Q   We had your mum up in the end. She came up with your Auntie Charlotte because we were so worried about you. And your mum said you were having nightmares at home.

L   I was. I used to burst out crying upstairs and everything.

Q   What was wrong?

L   Well it was like – right, they was all there sitting – and you said do this bit of work – and you're shaking – and you said write this story and I couldn't do it and I couldn't spell it and I was getting really, really worried – that's why I burst into tears – cos I couldn't do it – cos I was getting really, really worried cos I couldn't do it – I thought the others was gonna laugh if I never done it – that's why I burst out in tears.

Cos I always thought – I always wished – I wish I was brainy like the rest so I could write loads of stories out, you know, like RE and everything and you have to write sentences and I have to keep asking for spellings and everything – like this – and I just wish, you know, I could write it out – think of my ideas and everything – I can think of my ideas but I can't spell it . . .

The words printed on the page provide food for thought for all of us trying to help the Leslies of this world, but they fail to convey the real quality of our talks. Listening to the tapes I hear him giggle in places, exclaim in surprise, search desperately for the right words to express what he wants to say. At times the painful memories reduce him almost to a whisper. The transcript does though enable a number of points to be made concerning children who struggle to learn to read, points which have great implications for teachers of these children.

Histories

By the time I entered Leslie's life he had already a long history of failure. During the previous four years a number of adults had presented themselves as providers of help. In Leslie's eyes initially there must have been the hope with each of these that they would teach him how to read. I wonder at what point he ceased to believe? The problem with so much 'special needs' teaching is that so many faces become involved; so many ideas as to what to do. Which should he choose and whom should he believe? By the age of seven or eight he had obviously lost all faith in the system:

> I stopped reading – like you say don't stop reading well I stopped reading.
>
> I did all right but then I just dropped down.
>
> Cos I didn't think I'd learn.
>
> I just gave up.

It seems to me to be so important that we remember that the children we deal with come to us with just such histories and attendant memories. Before any work can be done a relationship must begin to develop, and this starts with a promise of time. Children like Leslie need to be told at the outset that a decent period of time will be available for the work together. In the middle school this was four years. Four years to aim at becoming a reader. Perhaps the most satisfying aspect of the transcript for me is its demonstration that after two years our relationship was such that Leslie felt able to confront his problems in this way and express himself so openly.

Emotions

It is not particularly original to say that children who fail respond to this failure emotionally, that they feel their failure deeply. However, it is still something of a shock to hear Leslie use words which convey vividly what he felt:

> I was really scared.
>
> . . . that's how it was – really scary.
>
> I was scared – cos I didn't know the words.
>
> . . . and you'd be scared and have to say 'I can't read it'.
>
> Well I was scared cos it was the headmistress.
>
> . . . and you're shaking . . . and I was getting really, really worried . . . that's why I burst out in tears.

Such feelings can only act as a block to learning and improvement. None of us would easily master a new skill if we felt this way, and we are confident adults with successful histories and high expectations. I am reminded of Leslie's words whenever I come across similar children in classrooms writing with their bodies wrapped over the page protectively so that no one can see. What hell it must be to have to hand that writing in. Until work is done to counter these feelings, any language work is liable to fall on deaf ears.

Methods

A fascinating aspect of what Leslie has to say is that he enables us to view approaches to reading and writing through the eyes of a child. At the beginning of this chapter I expressed my belief in the need to do this, to share our perceptions of our work with children and to encourage them to explore their thoughts and feelings. What Leslie says in no way detracts from the dedication and concern of the teachers who approached language work in the ways he refers to, but his view of what was going on was obviously somewhat different to theirs.

a. Reading till you get it right.

Both Leslie's record cards (quoted earlier) and his comments indicate that one teaching strategy was obliging a child to demonstrate mastery of a reading book before being given a new one. He had gone back to the beginning of the reading scheme as he had 'forgotten' previous work. The effect this had on Leslie is obvious.

> They kept giving you books over – like when you went onto a book, right, and you finish it and then you go onto another one the teacher would say if you can't read that one go back onto the other one – well I've read it again, so that's a bit boring . . . she's just giving you the same books.

> It was boring. They kept giving you the same books over and over again. That's why. I just gave up.

The recognition of the basic need to excite and motivate children with regard to their reading appears to have been absent from this teaching, and wouldn't we all get bored at reading the same books over and over again?

b. Colour coding.

The need to organize reading books into some sort of order or different levels is a feature of the vast majority of primary schools in this country. From the point of view of teachers it appears to make sense but such a decision will present children with a view of reading which will affect how they approach the business of learning to read. This argument is taken up in Chapter 3, for now we can see what Leslie made of it:

> there'd be green and blue and red and I was always on orange . . . that's me.

Though only a passing reference, this speaks volumes for the way in which our teaching methods influence children's views of themselves as readers. If Leslie was always on orange how was he ever going to behave like a 'real' reader? In addition it is sad that he remembers the colour coding but does not mention the titles of the books to be found at each level. If I am asked about books I have read recently I will answer with titles and authors and some idea of why I enjoyed them. I well remember a little girl in a school I was visiting who, when asked what books she had read recently, replied, 'green'!

c. Flash cards

Leslie's recollections of flash cards are very amusing and always raise a chuckle among teachers who listen to the tape of our conversations:

> Cos all the class used to say it. And I used to join in with that – if they started to say 'cu' I'd say 'cu' really quickly.

Again one has to question the sort of teaching strategy represented by what Leslie describes, but in addition this indicates something which children like him develop in order to cope with failure. The aim becomes not to ask for help, thereby admitting inadequacy, but to pretend that all is well. To lose oneself in the crowd, joining in so that no one will notice. This presents tremendous difficulties to teachers trying to help because it may not be at all obvious where help is needed most. Treating children in a class as a homogeneous collection ('The Class') and teaching them all in the same way is bound to create problems. The most cursory investigation of thirty 5-year-olds will reveal children at totally different levels of awareness and with differently developed skills with regard to reading and writing. Each one will require different help. Of course the hard-pressed infant teacher cannot possibly provide in such a way on her own, and this raises the issue of the place of other adults in the classroom – especially parents.

d. Reading to teacher

Leslie refers twice to reading aloud to his teachers and on each occasion makes me see the activity in a different light:

> [I read] . . . to the teacher most of the time – never by yourself – they never let you have a chance – they think, oh no, let's listen to him.

In my own mind (no doubt like most other teachers) I had always felt the need to provide extra time for the children who were struggling with their reading. This was a major strategy in the provision of help. I cared and demonstrated this caring by hearing them read as often as possible. Yet according to Leslie something very different was going on! Other children in the class were being left alone with their books to read silently, while he was picked on and forced to read to the teacher. Perhaps this is the most vivid demonstration in our conversations of the ways in which teacher and child view the same activity from different perspectives. Of course the attraction of being left alone is clear. Every reading session with me was a test of ability (in the child's eyes); a time when the failure stood clearly in the spotlight.

The second sort of reading session was to the headmistress and, again, the same points are worth making. Headteachers often offer themselves with all the best intentions to help with the poor readers. But Leslie was not so taken with the idea:

> Well I was scared cos it was the headmistress. So I tried as hard as I could not to get a word wrong cos it made me go all embarrassed.

The lovely description which follows of Leslie getting 'slower and slower' until he grinds to a halt, 'stuck on a word', and is encouraged to sound it out, ' "it's 'cl' Leslie, 'cl'." And I'd go, "cl . . . classroom!" ', again provokes smiles from teachers who hear it.

e. *Copying off the board*

Another common teaching strategy is specifically questioned by Leslie when he remembers early writing lessons:

> Copy off the board. Cos she writ everything on the board and what we had to do was copy it off – I reckon that was the problem – if I was the teacher I would've said 'write a story' – she just writ everything on the board and we had to copy, just copy.

I have head speakers on in-service courses refer to copying off the board in just this way! How much more effective to hear it from a child!

The need to help children develop as writers is an extremely important aspect of the work we do in school, but another comment of Leslie's made me question the sort of support and advice I was offering. He says:

> . . . she used to put a tick and one of them stars – and she used to put 'good' – but she never used to tell me if it was really good, you know, very good.

What I now call the 'tick-good syndrome' can be seen in exercise books in many primary schools. Often it is more than 'good', perhaps 'well done' or 'excellent', but in each case what is lacking is just what Leslie wanted: specific advice about the strengths and weaknesses of a piece of writing together with some idea of how to make it better next time. Which bits are 'good' or 'excellent'? Which bits could be better? How can I learn from my mistakes? If we want to really help children become confident and competent writers we must start offering real advice about their efforts.

A view of reading

Last, and perhaps most important in terms of the approaches recommended later in this book, is the view of reading held by Leslie. He demonstrates clearly that, despite the boredom and worry and poor self-image, he has been desperately searching for clues which might hold the key to reading success. All around him, certain types of books and teaching methods have been used and it is from them that he has built up ideas of what reading is and how he could learn to read. So he adopts a series of learning strategies which apparently will work:

That's what I kept doing – trying on the letters – oh, if only I could get this alphabet I could read all the words. But I didn't – I couldn't read all the words.

I did something else. Learn the words.

These two examples show Leslie desperately searching for a way forward. The alphabet seems to be important – all those flash cards and no doubt an alphabet frieze – so obviously this holds the key to success. But it did not:

So even when I learned the alphabet I couldn't do it. Funny ain't it really!

Leslie could not read and his teacher was helping him in particular ways, so these ways must provide the key to the problem. He was tested on his letters and so tried to learn the alphabet. Words were broken into sounds – so learn the sounds and blends. Words he did not know were written in a book – learn these for success. But, of course, none of these provided the answer. Reading does not work like that. So his theories failed and he gave up.

Leslie's view of reading can be discerned from the number of times he uses the words 'word', 'letter', 'sound' when he talks about it. He seems to see reading as a process of getting the words right and successful readers as people who are able to do so. When he reads aloud to a teacher this view is uppermost in his mind, and we can almost hear him say to himself, 'I must get the words right'. While thinking in this way he would never learn to read. Fluent, confident readers do not read to get the words right. They read to interact with what they are reading; to be informed, excited, moved. The fluent readers who are quoted in later chapters demonstrate this vividly. What I had to find was a method of reading which allowed Leslie to read like a fluent reader, unaware of the words and letters and concentrating on the meaning of what he was reading.

CHAPTER 2

The de-skilling of teachers

These Special Needs people, they tend to talk a different language, don't they.

> (Remark made by primary school teacher on an in-service course 4/11/86)

In general primary school teachers do not see themselves as having real expertise in the field of special needs. I am not saying that teachers do not have such skills and perceptions but that many do not think they have. Working with many teachers over the years and now visiting schools in a bigger area I have had the chance to see a wide diversity of practice and to talk to many teachers. The problem of whether a teacher sees herself as an 'expert' in a particular field, as possessing 'expertise', is often a crucial factor in determining the quality of work provided in the classroom. With regard to children who have reading and writing difficulties this is especially important. In classrooms, where such children are not being provided with real help designed to bring about improvement, it is often because deep down the teacher feels inadequate in this respect. I believe in fact that the best people to help such a child are his parents and class teacher because they know his background and his predicament better than anyone else. But special needs has become the province of the 'expert' and if these experts work in such a way as to make the class teacher feel inadequate, the child will suffer. I would like to explore some of the ways in which I think class teachers are 'de-skilled' in this area. They are based on remarks made constantly to me in conversation with both headteachers and class teachers. Together they form a rationale which has resulted in so much poor provision for the child with reading and writing problems in a mixed-ability classroom. It is a rationale based, I believe, on false premises.

'He can't concentrate'

This is perhaps the most common reason given to explain a child's lack of progress. Somewhere along the line reference has been made to 'concentration span' as being a crucial area affecting success or failure in learning. So when a child fails to concentrate on his reading or writing - seems uninterested in books and school work - this is fastened onto by the teacher. It is nothing to do with the school or teacher or the quality of work provided in the classroom; we are absolved from all blame. But this excuse is wrong for many reasons, the first of which hinges on a 'chicken-and-egg' type of argument. We can ask ourselves whether the lack of concentration is a cause of reading failure or a result? Put most of us in situations where we feel inadequate and are failing and we too will look for ways out. Could it be argued that the vast majority of 'poorly concentrating' reading failures do in fact possess more than adequate powers of concentration when faced with tasks that are intrinsically interesting? Certainly I have sat many such children down with beautiful reference and picture books to find them absorbed for long periods of time. Others will talk about hobbies and interests like model making or fishing which also require concentration. A major teaching strategy must then be to provide intrinsically interesting and relevant activities for these children: within reading and writing such activities as are advocated later in this book. In addition, work must be free from connotations of extrinsic failure or success. A child with a reading difficulty needs support in order to read the sorts of books which will provide their own motivation.

'He's dyslexic'

Or as one 8-year-old remarked to me recently when I asked if I could look at a story he was writing, 'It won't be much good because I've got dyslexia.'

The whole area of dyslexia is extremely contentious. Experts argue about its very existence while the media have accepted (why I wonder?) that the case is proven and that celebrity non-readers are 'dyslexic'. Faced with highly technical, difficult-to-read psychological books on the one hand and the media's total acceptance on the other (not to mention the private clinics sprouting up all over the country), is it any wonder that class teachers feel inadequate and reflect this inadequacy in the quality of their work?

Psychologists use the term 'developmental dyslexia' to decribe people who experience great difficulty with reading for no apparent reason. They are of average or high intelligence and do not appear to suffer from any physical, emotional or social handicap which would interfere with their learning. This term is used to distinguish such people from those who have suffered brain damage and thereby lost the ability to read - those who really are dyslexic. At first sight the description 'developmental dyslexia' appears harmless enough as a purely descriptive term, but in fact its use is fraught with problems. This is because the word dyslexia is bound to have connotations associated with its original use, that is brain damage or malfunction. So dyslexic children are commonly assumed to have something wrong with their brains. Three points need making about this.

Firstly one has to wonder why such an idea should be connected particularly with reading. We all display differing abilities in all sorts of areas, having to struggle with some. I find playing the piano extremely difficult, especially sight reading. The notation on the printed page does not transfer easily to my hands on the keyboard. This is despite two years of lessons and diligent practice. I do not believe I will ever be a fluent player, certainly not as fluent as many friends who appear to find the whole process easier to master. Should it be argued that my brain is not functioning normally? And what about my inability to beat primary school children at chess? Secondly the implications for the class teacher faced with a child described by a pyschologist as dyslexic can be very worrying. Is not the argument likely to be that if there is something wrong with his brain then surely one should not expect too much; and anyway it obviously requires particular expertise to deal with this child; there are specialist clinics which provide specialist help; you cannot expect me to know how to deal with what sounds like a medical condition? A poor scenario for the provision of any help. The third objection to this term lies in the implication that it is possible to discount all other factors which might have affected the child so that one is left only with dyslexia. Anyone who has ever worked with children who have reading difficulties knows that by the time they get to the age at which the problem makes itself apparent they have lived for six or seven years. Trying to unravel all of the factors which have contributed to the difficulty is extremely difficult in the easiest of cases and impossible in many. The closer you get to the child the more layers there are to unravel. Quite what does one make of the adult celebrities who are discounting many more years of failure in favour of the one magical condition that explains it all away?

The number of dyslexics is also confused by the many different conditions subsumed under the same umbrella. There are apparently children who have a colour problem and have learnt to read when provided with tinted spectacles. For other the print swirls into a blur and again particular spectacles have been found to help. But are these groups suffering from the same complaint? From a purely statistical viewpoint one would not expect every baby born to be physically perfect, so statistically some may well be born with kinds of perceptual problems which will later affect their ability to read (though that the great variety of problems so far identified should all be subsumed under the name of 'dyslexia' seems to me to be very questionable). However, would we really expect the numbers of such babies to explain the bulging 'remedial' departments in schools, the over-stretched special needs support teams and the rash of private clinics opening across the country? Surely not. Other factors, some educational and some social, seem to be responsible. Too many children fail to progress as readers and writers in schools, and parents would much prefer to have a dyslexic than an illiterate child.

The second point which needs to be made concerns the provision of work for such children. The basic premise of this book is that the approaches recommended will be of value to all children, be they fluent readers, slow readers, backward readers or 'dyslexics'. Therefore labels become redundant and irrelevant. Children who are failing as readers have special needs but do not necessarily require special teaching methods.

'He's disruptive/he lacks confidence'

So often I find myself faced with teachers commenting on the behaviour of children in terms which indicate that they see this as a reason for the failure to make progress. The aggressive behaviour or the passive acceptance of anything are opposite ends of a spectrum which results in reading problems. Of course there may well be pathological cases where such a prognosis is valid, but in most cases something very different is happening. Like the problem of concentration above, we have to ask whether the behaviour is the cause or the result of the problem. Children who early in their school careers fail to make progress while all around them others forge ahead, will initially become confused and then will look for ways of coping with the situation. Some become disruptive. Others retreat into themselves, accepting anything offered in a passive, non-thinking manner. Such coping strategies can be illustrated from the children who formed the group with Leslie. His behaviour has already been described - an initially nervous boy who retreated into tears and a 'can't do it' response to the situation. Others coped differently. Jennifer hit the school like an atomic explosion, rejecting everything we offered and appearing to have only one aim in life: to disrupt any of the classroom situations she found herself in! At the age of nine she was already an expert at causing chaos. She upset lots of people, both teachers and children, and it became a battle of wills to break this down and get to the real Jennifer underneath. Stephen was morose and very difficult to get 'close' to. Passing him in the corridor he would drop his eyes and stare intently at the floor (while Jennifer would shriek a raucous 'good morning!' to raise a laugh from classmates). Stephen's record cards spoke of him switching off in class, having a dreadful temper and constantly trying to 'get out of' classwork. His teachers did not appear to have had much time for him. Herbie was a placid, friendly boy with a ready smile - when he bothered to turn up for school! He had not learned to read for the simple reason that nobody had taught him. His father could not read and Herbie spent most of his time accompanying him on various jobs. He had no interest in learning to read and it did not appear to bother him one bit. Lastly there was Karl who had developed such a fear of the reading situation that it affected him physically. When reading to an adult his whole body would twist in what appeared to be great discomfort, his hands writhing in agony and his head nodding so vigorously that the print must really have been jumping up and down! He had only one strategy for 'working out' new words: phonics. So he religiously sounded out every word he came to. He had perfected this to such a degree that he now sounded out all the words, known or not! Very quickly, underneath his breath, the sounds would blur. And of course the result was nonsense. As I mention in Chapter 4, it was not until Karl began to admit to his feelings and talk openly about them that any progress was made with his reading. I could go on, seeing as I do in front of me a line of faces of children I worked with, all of them with their own ways of coping with the situation of failure. Once these coping strategies become established they are extremely difficult to break down, but if real progress is to be achieved then a breaking down must occur. The key will lie in that complex of relationships, intrinsic self-motivation and self-belief: not easy to achieve but certainly far more positive than seeing the behaviour as a reason for achieving nothing.

'He's got problems with his memory/visual discrimination/auditory discrimination/phonics ...'

I have grouped these together because they are the sorts of 'skills' tested by many diagnostic tests, and such tests are often used in this field. Weaknesses in any of them are taken to explain why the child is not making progress in reading. In addition work is often set to specifically improve such weaknesses. Such an approach has a very attractive simplicity which no doubt accounts for the faith many teachers place in it. But it is riddled with problems. Firstly one needs to stand back and take another common-sense view of what is implied by the notion that a weakness like poor memory is responsible for reading failure. Every day of their waking lives, children who cannot read demonstrate the adequacy of their memories. They remember all sorts of information necessary to lead 'normal' lives – names, whereabouts of things and places, times of events etc. In addition a short conversation is all that is required for them to demonstrate additional powers as they produce lists of television characters and pop stars or information about interests from pigeon racing to motorbikes (Leslie knew all about 'lamping' catching rabbits at night). If poor memory was really a factor then it would manifest itself in ways other than a diagnostic reading test. Or is it that many children appear to find 'remembering' difficult at school but no problem at home or in the street? And what does this mean?

The second major problem concerns the nature of reading. The sort of diagnostic test which isolates particular elements assumes that reading is essentially a 'static' process. Letters are visually recognized. Sounds are sounded. Words are decoded. But of course reading is not like that at all. It is a dynamic process in which a reader interacts with a text. This interaction involves the reader in bringing different awarenesses to the text – awarenesses about syntax, the nature of written language, life itself. Chapter 3 demonstrates what happens when a fluent reader engages with a meaningful text and Chapter 5 examines the implications for teaching. Suffice it to say at this point that reading is not about isolated skills.

The third problem follows from the last paragraph. Even if it was possible to break down a complex skill like reading into different components, it does not necessarily follow that we should teach these components in order that the skill be mastered. We must not make the mistake of arguing that because a poor reader does not know his sounds (poor phonic skills) we must teach him these sounds in order to turn him into a reader. The fallacy of this argument can be demonstrated by referring to two different skills: riding a bicycle and talking. In both of these cases the sub-skills involved are highly complex. What happens when we ride a bicycle might form the basis of a highly technical lecture by a physicist. How children learn to talk is studied in universities. But if we sat a novice bicycle rider down and explained the skills involved we would not be helping him to ride. What we actually do is sit him on the bicycle and provide support – we hold on until he is ready to go it alone (I believe we can apply just such a teaching method to children learning to read). Similarly no one sits a 2-year-old down and tries to explain about syntactic structure. Children learn the grammar of their native tongue. They are not taught. Like the bicycle rider they learn in a supportive environment, and they learn because they are highly motivated to learn. They realize that with language they can get things done. They learn that language is meaningful (again the implications for reading seem to me to be very important). They learn to talk because they are growing up in a society of talkers.

Lastly, the previous chapter in which Leslie talked about failing to learn to read demonstrates what happens when we concentrate on isolated 'bits' of the reading process. The thinking child perceives these bits as providing the answers to his problems. He desperately tries to learn them, thereby excluding other elements of the process. The result is liable to be further failure.

'He goes to Mrs X'

This is perhaps the saddest reason (from the child's viewpoint) for a lack of real help being provided in the classroom; perhaps, also, the most common way in which teachers are de-skilled in this field. Because the child with reading problems gets specialist help at certain times, the class teacher provides little or nothing. The child is being given 'specialist' treatment outside the classroom, about which the teacher knows very little. Perhaps the child returns to class with work to do – worksheets to fill in or puzzles to solve – so this is what he does. He is not thought capable of joining in many of the class activities. They are not for him. He goes to Mrs X. On many occasions I have heard members of special needs support teams talking to class teachers and asking such questions as, 'What would you like me to work on with him today?' The result is usually a somewhat puzzled look and a reply which, however it is phrased, really means 'Well don't ask me, you're the expert'.

The above list most certainly does not exhaust the reasons for children with reading and writing difficulties so often floundering in the classroom (for instance

I recently met a teacher who implied that she did not expect much from a particular child because she remembered teaching his father!) Neither is it intended as a negative criticism of primary school teachers. Feelings of uncertainty and inadequacy with regard to reading and writing problems are the result of teachers having been 'de-skilled'. This area has become the province of the 'expert' who has been trained to work in highly skilled ways. But class teachers need to be treated as experts, for only then will they see themselves as such. They need to realize that they are more than capable of providing for the children in their classes. They must trust themselves. Hopefully this book will enable such teachers to question what they do at present and to consider the approaches discussed in Chapter 6 as a way forward.

Before examining the sort of work I believe offers so much to children who have experienced difficulty learning to read I would like to consider two examples of work which I often find 'failing' children engaged on. How do many such children spend their time in the mixed-ability classroom? Of course much superb work is done, but it is not a feature of every classroom. When a teacher does not provide a rich working environment it is often due to feelings of not possessing the necessary expertise. Then one or the other of the following seems to occur.

'He enjoys filling in the worksheets'

What could be called the 'worksheet syndrome' lies like a suffocating blanket over so many failing children in primary classrooms. Duplicated worksheets concerned with the sorts of isolated skills discussed above are provided as a daily diet. Often they are left by over-worked members of special needs support teams as a way of providing continuity between weekly visits and helping the class teacher who wants 'suitable work'. But does anyone seriously believe that they really contribute to turning 'failed' readers and writers into children who can perform these skills fluently in a variety of situations and for different purposes? So, what are the problems?

The major criticism of the use of such materials has already been made earlier in this chapter. Reading and writing are not developed by working at isolated skills. In the classroom they should be 'real' activities concerned with 'real' books used for 'real' reading, and 'real' writing for 'real' purposes. So many commercially produced worksheets are excellent examples of the sort of artificial learning that can become a feature of a classroom if care is not taken. There is no reason why school learning and 'real' learning should be different, but they so often are. The major difference lies in the way real learning is not structured 'from above' as it were. We are surrounded by learning experiences all and every day which hit us in a haphazard fashion. It is the way we structure them, fitting them into our already existing knowledge, which brings about learning. The 'worksheet syndrome' means 'closed' tasks, highly structured, so that most chances for real thinking and real decision making are removed. The danger is that children with 'learning difficulties' are just those who are felt to be in need of a greater degree of 'structure' than 'ordinary' children. So they don't think. The task is already laid out in front of them with a set of instructions to follow. Success comes with following the instructions correctly. But this is not learning.

Once the above approach has been set in motion, further problems follow. The child, encouraged to behave in this passive, conditioned manner, completes the worksheets and is praised for so doing. This reward inevitably leads to the child who 'enjoys' filling in the worksheets. A closed task is safe and secure, no risks having to be taken, no danger of failure, and with a reward at the end. No wonder it is enjoyable. But real thinking and learning are not like that, and certainly not learning to read and write. Learning is a 'risk-taking' activity, involving the ability to test out new learning and see if it works. A real learning environment (which is surely what a classroom ought to be) should have an atmosphere in which real thinking goes on. It may not be so cosily 'enjoyable', but far more worthwhile (of course enjoyment is not a valid reason on its own for providing particular types of work – most children would 'enjoy' eating sweets all day!).

Two further points can be made when considering the use of published worksheets as part of a commercially produced programme. Firstly this approach to 'remedial' help exemplifies the way in which this field is seen to be the realm of the expert. Accompanying commercial schemes and other materials are ever larger and longer teachers' manuals explaining their use. Reading these, not only is the class teacher made to feel acutely ignorant of the issues involved but receives the distinct impression that without these materials there is little chance of any success being achieved. Mainstream reading schemes display this trend most dramatically – witness the manuals produced for the recent Oxford Reading Tree and Open Door. Yet nothing could be further from the truth. The class teacher, knowing her children, their environment and their learning needs is in the best position of all to provide for them. She knows better than any 'experts' producing materials for a mythical 'special needs child', what is required.

Secondly, so many commercial programmes are based on the premise that children with learning difficulties need to work in small steps within a tight structure. Could it be suggested that such an approach, owing its rationale to behaviourist psychology, might well be mistaken and that what many of these children need are not small steps but giant strides! Learning to read is not a linear experience proceeding from simple skills through to more complex. A learning reader does not travel from A to B in a straight line. In Chapter 4 a young girl's reading of a novel exemplifies the sorts of things which happen when any reader responds to a story. We have to read if we are to learn how to read. Children who see themselves as failures are just those who need to be shown how reading 'works' in practice. They need the same sort of support which would be provided for the novice bicycle rider. Many are confused (like Leslie in the first chapter) because of the different emphases which have been placed on particular sub-skills, for example sounds. More work on just these areas seems to be a recipe for further confusion and failure.

'He's my happy helper'

Just as the child laboriously filling in worksheets often seems happy and to be enjoying his work, so teachers see happiness as a prerequisite for the work they provide. It goes without saying that happiness and security are just what failing children need, but these in themselves are surely not sufficient. The 'happy' non-reader of 8 or 9 years of age all too soon becomes the disillusioned, morose non-reader of 14 or 15 and then the powerless, illiterate adult. The aim must be to effect improvement; the test of the work is the extent to which improvement is brought about. I have met 9-year-olds who have stated, 'I don't do the work that the others are all doing'. When asked what they do, it appears that drawing often takes up quite a lot of time. In addition they clear out cupboards, help put up displays, take registers to the office (or, in one case, the remedials always dug the long jump pit for Sports Day!): anything, it seems, except reading or writing. These are taught outside the classroom by Mrs X. It is often a great shock for such children to be re-involved with their classmates. But re-involved they must be if they are to learn to read and write. Initially they might not be so 'happy', although I have found this quickly fades as they realize just what they are able to contribute.

In this chapter I have tried to explore some of the reasons for children failing to make progress in the mixed-ability classroom. I must stress again that it has most certainly not been intended as a criticism of primary school teachers, but rather of the present situation in which I believe many of them feel unsure and insecure.

With regard to reading, the children we have been considering are those who because of their difficulties rarely show any interest in the world of books. They are the ones who fidget during silent reading, are forever changing their books, or who open their remedial reader on any page and then slump over it displaying that lack of interest to all. Then, all too soon, this reaction to failure is turned by the teacher into a reason: 'He can't read because he shows no interest in books'. But hand in hand with any reading instruction must be the development of such an interest. And all children will respond to books. All children will respond to the power of story. What we need is a way in for children who have been turned off by failure and who have never felt that wonderful losing of oneself in a story. Why should they be keen to read if they do not know what excitements reading has to offer?

In order to develop an approach which might help children respond to the world of books we will leave the strugglers for a time and look at two successes. In the next chapter a reading session with Jenny, a 4-year-old, is examined for clues to the reading process. Then in Chapter 4 we look at the reading of Sally, a fluent, experienced reader of 9. Both girls love stories and books. Perhaps if we can discover what they do when they read, clues might be offered as to the sort of help the failures need.

CHAPTER 3

Early Stages: Jenny, 4 years old, demonstrates the process

What's it say?

The focus of this chapter is on the early stages of learning to read. Many of Leslie's comments refer back to his days at the first school and seem to suggest that part of the reason for his lack of progress lay in what happened to him at that time. This is in no way meant to be a negative criticism of his teachers, who no doubt worried and worked hard to try and teach him how to read, but Leslie indicates that he found much of what happened puzzling. He tried to make sense of it but when he could not do so he gave up. Before long he saw himself as a failure and was frightened of the whole situation. Perhaps a consideration of how we might approach reading with young children could help prevent others becoming 'Leslies'. In order to examine early reading, a transcript of a reading session with a 4-year-old girl, Jenny, will be used. This will enable us to consider the nature of the reading process and the tremendous skills which young children bring to the business of learning to read. If teaching is about moving children on from what they can do, then surely we ought to use these skills as the starting point for our work in infant classrooms.

Like so many other confident 4-year-olds I found Jenny clutching her favourite book (*Goldilocks* in the Read It Yourself Ladybird series) and looking on me as someone to enjoy a book with! Had this been in a playgroup or nursery my chances of sharing the book alone with Jenny (let alone taping it) would have been slim indeed. My usual experience of such situations is that no sooner have I sat down on the carpet or easy chair or beanbag than I am being crawled over by eager children all wanting to hear (and contribute to) the story! Such is the power of narrative! However, Jenny was at my house, being the daughter of friends, so I had her to myself. She was totally unconcerned by the tape-recorder and if anything it made her more willing to read. Certainly she was fascinated when I played the tape back to her. We settled ourselves down, Jenny opened the book on the first page and:

Jenny ONCE THERE WERE THREE BEARS. THIS IS DADDY BEAR. THIS IS MUMMY
BEAR. AND THIS IS . . . LITTLE BEAR, TINY BEAR, LITTLE BEAR.

Me He is little bear. Look at him.

J THE THREE BEARS WENT FOR A WALK.

M They did!

J What does that say?

M Who's that do you think?

J Goldilocks.

M That's right! What's she doing?

J GOLDI . . . what's it say?

M HERE IS GOLDILOCKS

J HERE IS GOLDILOCKS. What's she doing?

M She's going inside their house.

J Goldilocks, you know, she's very hungry because, you see, because she
hasn't eaten any breakfast. SHE TRIES THE DADDY BOWL. IT'S, IT'S, IT'S TOO
. . .

M The daddy bowl's – what's wrong? It's too salty. Ugh!

J IT'S TOO SALTY. SHE TRIES THE MUMMY BEAR'S. IT'S TOO SWEET. THEN SHE
TRIES THE BABY BEAR'S PORRIDGE. IT'S JUST RIGHT.

M It is! So what does she do?

J SHE EATS IT. SHE TRIES SOME MORE. What's it say?

M Now what's she doing?

J Sitting in the chair.

M Whose chair is that do you think?

J I think that's Daddy Bear's chair.

M Right. Looks a bit hard to me.

J GOLDILOCKS SITS ON DADDY BEAR'S CHAIR. IT'S TOO HARD. THEN SHE SITS
ON MUMMY BEAR'S CHAIR. IT'S TOO SOFT. THEN, THEN, THEN, what's it say?

M She sees . . .

J SHE SEES BABY BEAR'S CHAIR. THEN IT IS JUST RIGHT. All Baby Bear's things
are just right!

M They are aren't they! But what happens to Baby Bear's chair?

J THEN . . . THEN IT IS . . . then it broke!

M Oh dear she has broken his chair!

J That's because she's too big. Perhaps she's seven or eight.

M Perhaps she is. Do you think she'd be all right if she was four like you?

J Well I think she'd be all right if she was one or two. Something like that.

M Do you think?

J Yes, because you see Baby Bear he could be one or two couldn't he?

M Yes, I reckon he might be one or two.

J Yes because . . . GOLDILOCKS WANTS TO GO UPSTAIRS. SHE GOES UPSTAIRS.
THEN SHE TRIES DADDY BEAR'S BED. IT IS TOO HARD. Is it too hard?

M Yes, looks a bit hard to me, doesn't it?

J SHE LIES ON DADDY BEAR'S BED. IT IS TOO HARD. THEN SHE LIES ON MUMMY

BEAR'S BED. IT IS TOO SOFT. SHE TRIES BABY BEAR'S BED. IT IS JUST RIGHT.

M   Look, Goldilocks has gone to sleep.

J   Yes! THE THREE BEARS COME HOME. BABY BEAR LOOKS AT HIS TINY CHAIR. LOOK! A GIRL HAS BROKEN MY CHAIR, HE SAYS. AND SHE'S ATEN MY PORRIDGE. THE THREE BEARS GO UPSTAIRS. DADDY BEAR'S . . . HERE SHE IS! HERE'S THE NAUGHTY GIRL THAT'S BROKEN MY CHAIR AND ATEN MY PORRIDGE. HERE SHE IS. THEY THROW HER – THEY THROW HER DOWNSTAIRS. SHE RAN OUT.

M   Do you think she ever went back there again?

J   Yes because you see I know another story and they threw her downstairs and she was hurt.

M   Was she? And what did she do after that?

J   Oh well, she died!

As with any transcript, what is lacking is a clear indication of the quality of the conversation in terms of intonation. Whenever I listen to the tapes of Jenny or Leslie what gives them their 'life' is the real voice of a real person. To hear Leslie struggle to find the words which appear so easily on the printed page or Jenny's utter delight in the story of Goldilocks gives one so much more than any reading of a transcript. Nevertheless, just as Leslie's words make us think about reading failure, so the above reading session enables us to consider what Jenny knows about reading and what she brings to the books she loves. It is a window onto the reading process. How best to help Jenny develop as a reader should surely be based on what she can do at the moment.

Jenny's skills and awarenesses will be considered under two headings.

1 Oral skills

By the age of 4 (to be exact, four years one month) Jenny has learnt to talk! This might appear a rather obvious observation to make but it is important in two different ways. Firstly she brings her ability to understand and compose language to her reading and secondly she brings the learning strategies which have worked so well in enabling her to learn. With regard to the former, without a knowledge of the grammar of English it would be impossible for Jenny to make any sense of the story she was reading. One of the ways in which readers make their ways through texts is by being able to predict the sorts of words which can occur in different parts of sentences. The sentence:

She kicked the ball through the —

can only have certain classes of words completing it; a noun (window or door) or an adjective (big or glass). A verb, such as walking, would result in an ungrammatical sentence.

She kicked the ball through the walking.

Jenny 'knows' this in much the same way we do. If she did not, then she would not be able to talk and converse in a meaningful way. She would not be able to understand what I was saying to her and would not be able to compose her own sentences. She certainly would not be able to relate the story of Goldilocks.

There is also a very nice example in the transcript of another aspect of Jenny's language development which not only displays her awareness of English grammar but also offers a clue to the way she has gone about learning it. She uses the word 'aten' twice (very clearly when the tape is listened to) for 'eaten'. Why should she do this? The reason is that Jenny has not been sitting back for the past four years, passively being taught to speak. She has in fact, like every other 4-year-old, been very active. She has been determined to make sense of the environment, the situations and the people around her. A major drive has been to make sense of the language surrounding her and then to try out what she has learnt to make further progress. Through the grammatical errors she makes we see her experimenting with the rules which govern English. 'Aten' is wrong, just as 'runned' and 'swimmed' are wrong, but it is not difficult to see why young children should make such mistakes. Such a learning strategy is obviously enormously successful – just think what she has achieved in the few years of her life so far – but in order for it to succeed a number of conditions are necessary.

Firstly Jenny had to be in an environment which made sense. She had to experience spoken language in situations that were meaningful to her. Growing up in her family she was surrounded by other people (especially the people who were important to her) using language constantly. They would talk to each other, and, more important, they would talk to her. From the first few days of her life, her parents would have been talking to her, responding to the sounds she made and the changing expressions on her face. And a major reason for their great interest would have been the tremendous desire to communicate with their child. That would have been the aim: communication. Parents do no sit their children on their knees and give them talking lessons! When Jenny finally came out with the magic sounds 'ma-ma', her mother did not rush off to tick this off on a phonetic check list! 'Darling, she's learnt her 'm' sound.'

As Jenny got older, the conversations between herself and her parents would have been concerned with the things happening around them. It was in order to express her thoughts and feelings about these things that she strove to work out how to talk in English. Her parents spoke English and so she wanted to join in. She wanted to be like them. In addition she would have begun to realize the great power language was giving her in her everyday life: the power to make her wants known to her parents, to express her feelings etc. We learn language because of what it enables us to do with it.

The above points concerning Jenny's oral language development have real implications for approaches to reading. They mean that we ought to harness her tremendous drive to make sense of situations that she finds herself in. She has spent four years making sense of the world around her and now needs reading matter which again makes sense. The story of Goldilocks certainly does mean something to her, and the importance of story is discussed in detail below. But growing up in Britain in 1987 she will have learnt quickly that the peculiar squiggles all around her have meaning. She will have seen them in shops and on packets and tins, in magazines and newspapers and on the television. And she will have seen her parents and others making meaning out of them. She will have asked about them just as she did in Goldilocks ('What's it say?') and will have had her questions answered. Her parents will have drawn her attention to them on road signs, street names, shop fronts etc. In the same way she will certainly expect to make sense of what her first teacher does with her in terms of reading at school. She will also expect to be able to use the extremely successful learning strategies which have worked so well up to now. She will make mistakes as she tries things out and when she is puzzled she will expect to be able to ask for help, 'What's it say?' She needs an interested reader with her, sharing the story, just as she has shared so many domestic activities at home previously and learnt to talk by talking about them. It is by reading, with help, that she will learn to read. The making of mistakes (the taking of risks) is fundamental to this learning, just as she makes mistakes still with her speech ('aten'). In the same way that it would have been totally nonsensical for her parents to have tried to structure her oral language development by teaching her sounds followed by words followed by sentences, so such a strategy must be equally nonsensical to most 5-year-olds when applied to reading. What her parents did do was to provide experiences within which language was used quite naturally, and the focus of everyone's attention was on the experiences. Talk happened as part of them. So the attention of children learning to read should be on the meaning of what they are reading. Our job is to help them read it.

However, in one important way we need to be very careful about harnessing Jenny's impressive oral ability. It has been argued (very recently in the case of the Open Door reading scheme) that because children have learnt to speak, so the early texts they are given to read should be close to speech (Open Door uses speech bubbles). The problem with such an approach is that it may well clash with a very strong expectation children like Jenny must have concerning the language of their early reading books. Furthermore it does not allow them to use their knowledge of this language. Oral language and written language are different and Jenny is already aware of this. Just what exactly is it that she knows?

2 Story skills

The second major area of skills and awarenesses which Jenny has developed at home and which she brings to the task of learning to read involves writing, and more specifically stories. Later in this book I will argue for the use of stories with older children as a way to reading, and of the importance of story as a fundamental way in which we think. Just as we use stories (the tales we tell each other) to bring some order to the events which make up our lives, so fictional stories have a universal appeal. Jenny, like any other young child who has grown up with story books, is obviously already hooked. The story of Goldilocks means a great deal to her. Given that she has already experienced the power of story many times, as her parents have read to her, and has already acquired a repertoire of favourites, does it not seem obvious that this should be used in the initial stages of learning to read? Indeed, that it should form the basis of how she in fact develops as a reader? We, as teachers, know full well the tremendous power of story whenever we are reading aloud to a group of children and a particularly dramatic incident occurs. An electric atmosphere develops in the room; a silence and an intensity in the eyes of the children; looks of open-mouthed amazement on their faces. We feel the intensity and should realize that we are engaging with something very special here. It does not occur in maths or science or PE. It is something that goes beyond these, deep into our innermost beings, into the unspoken feelings and thoughts which we all share and yet which each one of us experiences uniquely. There are very good reasons why every culture has its own collection of folk tales which have lasted over many generations, and why certain modern stories (Sendak's *Where The Wild Things Are* is a good example) seem to touch so many children in the same way. Story should surely be used as the way into reading for young children, for stories are what they want to read.

As children listen to stories being read to them in the years before they go to school, not only do they become hooked on them and the books in which they appear, but they begin to build up knowledge of how they work and the language in which they are narrated. In order to fully appreciate what they know, I must now reveal something about Jenny's reading of Goldilocks. She did not read a word of it. She is a non-reader. She made her way through the book by looking at the pictures and remembering a story she has shared with her parents many times. In so doing she demonstrates what she knows about story in general. Firstly she knows the difference between talking about stories and 'reading' them. In the transcript the parts where she is 'reading' are printed in capital letters, but when listening to Jenny these parts are obvious. Her whole way of speaking changes as she puts on her 'reading voice'. Yet how different from the reading voices of so many children trying to read about Peter and Jane or Roger Red Hat. A better description of the way Jenny uses her voice would be a 'story-telling voice', for it is full of expression and intonation and excitement. She is pretending to read but she knows that reading aloud is all about performing. She has a dramatic tale to tell and must tell it dramatically. The reading voices of too many children, especially those like Leslie who fail, are not like this at all. A dull, monotonous drone would sum them up. There are two reasons for this, the first one being that the child's view of reading aloud to teacher is nothing to do with telling dramatic stories. If the teacher is marking the register at the same time or explaining a maths work card to another child or telling other children to sit down or stop talking or getting up and leaving the reader droning on alone or listening to two children read at the same time, what messages are being transmitted about what reading means? Children quickly learn the hidden curriculum of the classroom and work out how to behave in the appropriate ways. The second reason for the expressionless reading voice is the quality of the text being read. You can only read with excitement and intonation (that is, turn the reading into a performance) if what you are reading allows you to do so. Try reading most of the books which make up the reading schemes on the market today. They defy attempts at dramatic reading. Putting excitement and intonation into the reading makes the reader sound like an imbecile! But, of course, they are not designed to be read in this way. They are not about the power of story. They justify themselves in terms of a mythical structure and progression of 'skills' introduced in small steps. They have been worked out by 'experts' so that the teacher can feel safe about letting the scheme do the work.

A child's knowledge of story can be demonstrated in another way. Christopher, also aged 4, was invited to write a story with me. We were a partnership: he would make the story up and I would write it down. This is what he dictated:

> Once upon a time there was a witch and she had a broomstick. She could not find her broomstick so she got on a horse and galloped away. When she went to the party she wore a big black cloak, pair of shoes, striped socks and legs. She ate jelly and ice cream and crisps. All her friends sat at the table and then she went back home and had her lunch. Then she went to bed and when she got up next morning she had her breakfast quickly and then she went to another party.

It has to said that Christopher did not find this task easy and there were long pauses between some of the sentences. He did not simply dictate it as easily as it appears when written down. Given that, what is to be made of his story? Firstly it is recognizably a story, with a formal opening, and a plot. There is not much of an ending (certainly nothing as dramatic as Jenny's 'Oh well, she died!') but Christopher had put a lot of effort into the story and appeared to have had enough by the time he reached what became the ending. Secondly it is about a story character, a witch, the sort of stock, conventional character who will have appeared in the stories Christopher has grown up with. No doubt he will expect to find such characters in the books he is given to read at school. Thirdly, and perhaps most importantly, the story is told in story language, Christopher demonstrating at a very early age his ability to distinguish between written and spoken language. The many stories he has listened to have enabled him to internalize the structures and rhythms of the language of writing. From the 'Once upon a time' opening through the description of the witch and what happens to her, Christopher is using written language. He would not speak like this.

The knowledge Jenny and Christopher possess of the grammar of English, together with their awareness of the way stories are narrated, should surely give them a great start when they begin to learn to read. However this will only happen if the written texts they are given enable them to use what they know.

Too many of the books supposedly produced to aid 'the teaching of reading' are written in a language which does not allow learner readers to begin to predict their way through them. Indeed the language of some is so strange as to defy any sort of prediction, and quite what 4- and 5-year-olds make of the 'language' of flash cards and work sheets is anybody's guess. The fact that so many children learn to read successfully only goes to show how determined they are to make sense of reading.

Finally Jenny and Christopher enable us to focus on what happens when readers read stories. This area, reader-response, is developed later with the fluent 9- and 10-year-olds, but here the point needs making that all readers and listeners interact with stories. We bring ourselves to the story and constantly make connections between what we are reading and our own lives. In the transcript of Jenny 'reading' Goldilocks there are a number of examples of this:

J   Goldilocks, you know, she's very hungry because, you see, because she hasn't eaten any breakfast.
M   Oh dear she's broken his chair!
J   That's because she's too big. Perhaps she's seven or eight.

Similarly Christopher's story with its references to friends, parties and eating is obviously based on important areas of his life. If our aim is to make learning to read easy and if, at the same time, we want children to develop a love of reading and books so that they continue to read once they have learnt, we need to bring books and readers closer together. We must share with them our excitement about books and stories. We must harness the power of story. In classrooms where teachers are committed to such an approach the strength of the argument is plain to see. A range of picture books is displayed around the room and these books are openly accessible to the children. A child chooses a reading book, knowing that the teacher or parents will want to share it. Sometimes the teacher will read and the child will follow, sometimes they will take it in turns to read bits, sometimes they will read together in unison, sometimes the child will take the lead and the teacher will only join in if the child begins to struggle. Often all of these things and others happen at home and at school over a period of days with the same book. Always there is the encouragement to stop and react to what is being read, to laugh and to wonder, to examine the pictures, to consider what might be going to happen next. No one can prescribe how to share a book with a child. The best advice is simply to make sure you both enjoy it. In addition to this 'shared reading' there is time every day for the children to enjoy books quietly on their own or with a friend. Reading is best done silently and at the reader's own pace. Reception children love being left alone with books. Similarly every day the teacher reads aloud to the class, not as some sort of light relief at the end of the day after the 'important' business of maths and language has made everyone tired and ready for home, but to build on the five years that have gone before and to develop the knowledge and motivation necessary for reading success.

Whenever a reader reads, two elements are involved: the reader and what is being read. The history of the teaching of reading has been, until recently, concerned mainly with the latter and there have been many ideas about how written language can be 'simplified' in order to make it easy for a young reader to read. The argument has been that the English language is complicated and children must therefore have specially prepared texts written for them. Given that it is obvious young, learner readers would gain very little from *War and Peace* or *Wuthering Heights,* exactly what sort of text they do require needs careful consideration. Jenny has shown us that. The search for a successful method of teaching reading through the supposed simplification of language has been based all too often on false premises. One approach, still found today, has argued that because letters and words are 'simpler' than stories (and the sentences that make up stories), children should learn letters and words before they graduate to stories in books. A different approach has emphasized the complexity of the sound-symbol relationships in the English language, so that texts are written in which these are introduced in a graded way (with plenty of repetition to assist children's learning: 'Pat had a hat on the mat'). Neither of these takes into account the sorts of skills and knowledge displayed by Jenny and Christopher. This is not to denigrate the efforts of those in the past who have worked so hard to find the best ways of helping children learn to read. It is just to indicate that in their concentration on the language many lost sight of how it is used and the children who use it.

Such methods (and there have been others!) attracted teachers convinced of their worth, while others hedged their bets by using a combination of them. Arguments have raged between the proponents of the different approaches. And throughout all of this the vast majority of children have quietly gone on learning to read. Having listened to Jenny, we now have clues as to how they may have managed to do so. It is not (as I have heard stated) that 'Any method of teaching reading works', but that children use their skills, knowledge and tremendous drive to make sense of their world, to learn for themselves. Perhaps only those like Leslie who fail to make progress go searching amongst the strategies employed in their classrooms for the key which will bring them success.

We need to distinguish, then, between teaching and learning in the sense that we cannot assume children learn to read as a result of the teaching methods employed by their teachers. Teachers teach and children learn but there may be not much connection between them! Rather than treat children as blank slates on which we can work we need to consider how we can build on the skills, awarenesses and expectations which they bring to the reception classroom. Children learn a lot in the first five years of life! What they learn and how they go about learning should provide the rationale for the early stages of learning to read. Approaching reading in this way results in a definite shift in our concerns, away from trying to teach and towards considerations of the environment and experiences most likely to facilitate learning. As a result the role of the adult – teacher or parent – has to be considered, as well as the sorts of reading materials to be provided.

In our desire to simplify the task of learning to read the emphasis has for too long been on the language in the books to be read rather than on the reader who will read it. From an adult perspective (and even more from the perspective of language and reading experts) the ways in which English can be 'simplified' may indeed appear obvious, and when these are combined with a view of learning based on a controlled accumulation of knowledge in small, structured steps, the reasoning behind the many different methods of teaching reading becomes clear. Reinforcement is provided by controlled repetition of vocabulary and motivation by getting through the scheme as quickly as possible. But children do not see things through the perspective of reading experts and must make their own sense of it in their own ways. This chapter has tried to demonstrate what they do know about reading, skills and knowledge which are built up through stories at home. The mistake has been to think of reading as getting the words right, and to think that we do this by combining the sounds of letters. Jenny demonstrates that we come to the words (and letters) through texts that mean something. We read stories and in doing so learn how to read words. All learner readers need are books worth reading and adults who want to share them. Within the classroom the teacher should be concerned primarily with organizing an environment and experiences which produce in children a desire to want to read. Reflecting the literate environment in which children grow up through the use of all sorts of written materials, messages and instructions which NEED to be read will be a major part of this. Reading and writing work together in the development of literacy. But at the heart of learning to read will be the world of story and the books in which tales are told. If the children grow up with stories at home then the motivation will come from within. They will want to read these stories for themselves.

CHAPTER 4

How Sally solved the mystery of Tom's Midnight Garden

In order to love or hate something which exists only as a series of signs made with printer's ink, the reader must endow it with a phantom life, an emanation from his conscious or unconscious self.

(Arthur Koestler 1964)

Literature begins with the telling of a tale.

(Arthur Koestler 1964)

In this chapter we are going to consider fluent, confident readers: children who have learnt to read without any conscious thought at all and who love books and reading. The reasons for this are crucial to an appreciation of the methods of working described in later chapters, which recommend a fundamental re-think of approaches to children with reading difficulties. They are the principles upon which such work is based. Firstly we must consider the nature of the motivation which turns so many children into avid readers. Just what is the attraction in reading all of those books? Why do I as an adult enjoy reading? Secondly we must examine just what it is that fluent readers do when they are engaged with a written text. Exactly how are they finding their way through the printed marks on the page? I will argue that working with children who are having difficulty learning to read should involve providing the support necessary for them to behave as real, fluent readers; to begin to do unconsciously what they have been struggling to do consciously. Fluent readers are not conscious of the actual words on the page but of the ideas and feelings which lie behind the words. Work which continues to focus the reader's attention on surface features such as words, letters or sound-symbol relationships is not concerned with fluent reading. Young children learn to read stories not words. In addition books must be used which are powerful enough to affect the reader, thereby providing the motivation for reading more of them. How many of the reading books specially designed for 'remedial' readers are able to do this?

What I came to realize and am now firmly convinced of is that a major strategy in the provision of 'remedial' help should be the reading and discussion of literature. This is not to deny the use of other approaches, for instance the print surrounding children both in and out of school should be a major resource. Indeed the desire to make sense of this print and to be able to join in with adults and older children who can do so is a fundamental reason for many children learning to read. But literature – the telling of tales – has a universal human appeal. Stories are a basic, human characteristic. From earliest times people have told stories and listened to others telling them. They have expressed their thoughts, emotions and beliefs in story form from time immemorial: the creation stories, parables, mythologies from all over the world, ballads, folk tales and fairy tales. Always there have been stories. Our own lives have their beginnings, middles and ends; their distinctive plots in which different characters appear and disappear. It would seem that stories are part of being human. The power of story can be observed in very young children. It does not have to be taught. If a young child does not enjoy listening to a story well told then there is something wrong. It is not by chance that thousands of children have stories read to them every evening before they go to sleep. The appeal is basic. Those who are read to regularly often seem never satisfied, demanding more and more stories, while at the same time returning to particular favourites over and over again. It is the desire to constantly re-enter the world of story that lies behind the avid reading of so many children and adults. If 'failed' readers are denied access to this world, a major motivational force is not being used by those trying to help them.

How one could work with imaginative literature with children who have reading difficulties will be explored in the next chapter. Now the attention fixes on a 10-year-old-girl, Sally, and her reading of *Tom's Midnight Garden* by Philippa Pearce. In discussing how she made her way through this novel the idea is not to focus on how she read the words on the page at all. Indeed I have no idea how she did so as the reading was done silently at home in her own time. What sort of 'miscues' she made is not known and is totally irrelevant. What I was interested in was how she read the story Philippa Pearce had written – a very different concern to the words on the page. The work of such 'reader-response' literary critics as Wolfgang Iser is extremely interesting in focusing on what readers do when they read novels. I have argued that children should read for meaning. Such meaning is traditionally referred to as 'comprehension', so that we try and ensure that children have comprehended what they have read. In *The Act Of Reading* (1978) however, Iser takes us a step further from this view of reading by arguing that it is a mistake to view the meaning of a novel or story as residing solely within that text. The meaning of a text does not just lie in the words on the page but is the result of an interaction between the reader and what is written. A reader then is not passively accepting meaning from a text but is actively engaged with it. The words on the page will lead the reader in certain directions but the reader brings a great deal of himself to the reading.

So, what exactly is going on when a reader sits down to read a novel? When the idea of literary critics such as Iser are considered what we find is something that most readers would recognize. Certainly that was my reaction – yes, I read like that! He sees the reader as being engaged in a constant movement between looking back at what has happened and looking forward to what might be about to happen. As we read we store away in our minds what we think is important and this will affect our predictions for the future. We are affected by the characters and the twists of the plot, by the narrator from whose perspective the story is being told. And we bring ourselves to the reading: our life experiences, opinions, beliefs. We really are 'active' as we read! (If this is what reading is all about, where on earth do those comprehension exercises, using extracts from novels, fit in?)

In order to examine how readers read, Sally was given a copy of *Tom's Midnight Garden* and asked to read as much or as little as she wanted each night until she had finished. In fact it took her nine evenings to complete the novel and every morning she described what she was thinking and feeling about the previous evening's reading. Sally clearly displays how she was responding to the novel while she was reading it. What she said confirms many of the ideas proposed by Iser concerning reader-response. In addition it seems to have important implications for classroom approaches to the teaching of fiction and forces us to consider exactly what sort of reading with what sort of texts we should be doing with children who have reading difficulties.

On the first evening she read the first four chapters:

I guessed by the picture on the front that he met somebody, and it might have been the maid that he saw the evening before . . . Mrs Bartholomew doesn't seem normal, she's all dressed in black and her character doesn't seem normal . . . creeping about keeping something away from everyone. I think it's something to do with Mrs Bartholomew and perhaps she's got a ghost or something and it's all magical, but I'm not sure yet.

The next day Sally had read a further three chapters:

Well I still haven't found out who made the footprints but I've found some clues. Tom had found a letter and it was addressed to the king of the fairies and it gave me a bit of a clue that it might have been something to do with the fairies in the garden . . . I think it's something to do with Mrs Bartholomew now because she's got the clock, and up in her room Tom saw the maid dusting and there was somebody else in the room and he couldn't see who it was . . . I hope he'll meet this girl and they'll find something – I don't know what . . . I hope they'll discover something that will explain it all.

Two days later Sally had moved on from Chapter 7 to Chapter 12:

Well I've found out whose the footprints are. It's Hattie who's somebody in the house in the garden at midnight . . . I want to know a bit more about the village that Tom's seen once . . . because I think she's meant to be the princess of that village and he isn't sure about that and neither am I really. She says she's in disguise but she doesn't really act like a princess. She seems to be a bit common, she's more like any girl.

A further two days later Sally had finished Chapter 16:

I think Hattie's a princess now . . . her mother and father have been killed and she's been taken in by this lady who's been looking after her . . . she doesn't take much care of her . . . I don't know why she doesn't really like Hattie . . . her and Tom have an argument about who is the ghost. I think it's Hattie. I think in the end it will be something to do with the village. Tom's going to find out that the aunt is Mrs Bartholomew, because she's an old lady and so is the aunt.

During the next two days Sally had read a further six chapters and now had incorporated the words on the grandfather clock into her theory:

I definitely think it's something to do with Mrs Bartholomew and the clock because everyone's grown and the last time Tom saw Hattie's aunt she was much older too and Mrs Bartholomew's very old and so I think either the aunt or her ancestors could be her.

Asked if the aunt could still be alive in the present, Sally replied:

I don't know, unless it was something to do with the time. 'Time No Longer' could mean that she's connected with the clock and it means that she's got to a certain age and she can't go any further because time has stopped for her.
   What about Tom getting thinner?
   Well, it could mean that because he's something to do with a ghost in the garden, because it wasn't his time, it could mean that Hattie doesn't see him quite clearly . . . he's fading away, she must be getting older and so she doesn't believe quite so much in him. Well, she does, but she doesn't believe in the same sorts of things now as she's much older.

On the final morning, Sally had finished the novel and was able to see how her predictions had worked out:

Well I've found out that Mrs Bartholomew was Hattie and she had been dreaming of when she was young and Tom had somehow been able to get into her dreams and recently she had been thinking of it so Tom hadn't been able to get in. She'd been thinking of her husband instead . . . I didn't think she was Hattie until right at the end when Tom screamed and Mrs Bartholomew asked for him to apologize. That gave me a clue . . . I was a bit disappointed that Tom wouldn't be able to go back in the garden afterwards with Peter . . .

Sally's reading of *Tom's Midnight Garden* clearly shows the way in which her hopes and expectations formed a major part of the enjoyment she obviously experienced. In fact, nearly all of her predicting turns out to be wrong but much of the pleasure she gained from her reading lay in just such hypothesizing and wondering and modifying of ideas as the plot unfolded. And this is much more than just a desire to predict what happens next, for what Sally is actually doing is constantly attempting to organize the novel so that the different strands will fit together. In doing this she has to decide what is important in terms of its contribution to the overall structure and what is not so significant. She considers fairies in the garden, the village, Hattie as a princess of the village and 'Time No Longer' (which she interprets 'wrongly'). She realized the importance of Mrs Bartholomew very early on in her reading, but did not guess her identity until the end. She failed to appreciate the significance of some sentences early in the novel – for instance in Chapter 4 the reader is told that Mrs Bartholomew 'was dreaming of the scenes of her childhood' – but as an adult experienced reader so did I! Sally's ability to read in this way is due to the fact that she has read a number of novels before and is beginning to realize how novels 'work'. Her reading of novels has shown her how to read. She is becoming a reader by reading.

The reader, then, is actively engaged with the text in the search for meaning rather than being passively acted upon by what he is reading, so that different readers will read the same novel in different ways. The significance a novel has for a reader will be personal, varying from reader to reader, though limited by the text itself. Sally's reading certainly is personal – other readers would no doubt form different hypotheses. The text guided her in certain directions but her reactions came from within herself as she tried to make sense of what was happening.

Another of Iser's ideas which most readers would recognize is the way in which the words on the page become converted into images or 'pictures in the mind'. I certainly do this as I read, and if asked to think about a novel I have read, always find myself seeing a vague picture of some scene which obviously affected me. As we read, so the images change as we build up information from the writing and we discard the old in favour of the new. In Iser's view these particular images are not to be confused with images formed in the mind when we perceive objects. If I look at a dog and then close my eyes, the picture in my mind will look like the dog. But writing is not as precise as that. We will all interpret the words in our own ways, and the words could not possibly give us the same detail as we get when we are able to look at what is being described. So you could say that the images are produced from clues in the text, the reader filling in the missing parts and constantly modifying them. Again, readers are really active as they read, bringing so much of themselves to the reading. Different readers will form different images and Iser refers to the reactions of people to filmed versions of novels in which they are presented with 'complete' pictures of characters and settings. These often prove dissatisfying in that they do not correspond to the images formed from the reading.

At various times during her reading Sally was asked to close her eyes and explain what was happening in her mind when she thought about the novel. She was not asked what she could 'see' but interestingly she always described pictures, as in the following conversation.

Sally   I see Tom going downstairs.
Q   Do you see a picture or the words on the page?

S   No, I see a picture. I'm looking at the whole room, with Tom over in the one corner and the grandfather clock by him just as he's touching it. Then the maid comes in. I'm looking through something, being able to see him.

Throughout the conversations Sally made it quite plain that she 'saw' the scenes she was reading. However, her descriptions were always vague; rooms being described as 'old fashioned' and people as 'tall' or 'slim'. It was difficult to determine whether this vagueness was attributable to the images themselves or to her difficulty in describing them but it seemed clear that her pictures of Tom, Hattie and the garden must be personal (though no doubt influenced by the illustration on the front cover!).

The filling in of missing parts of a text – the 'gaps' that the author leaves – is not confined to images formed in the reader's mind. In sorting out what is happening and attempting to organize it the reader is constantly dealing with the gaps in the text. Many of Sally's comments above, describing her reading, are her reactions to what she has not been told. Through this process Sally really does become actively engaged with the text, demonstrating how much a reader contributes to the reading. The author cannot give her the whole picture at once and so she is constantly filling in the missing elements: '. . . but I've found some clues . . .', 'I want to know a bit more about the village . . .', 'I don't know why she really doesn't like Hattie . . .', 'I definitely think it's something to do with . . .', Iser (1978) comments:

> No tale can be told in its entirety. Indeed it is only through inevitable omissions that a story will gain its dynamism. Thus whenever the flow is interrupted and we are led off in unexpected directions, the opportunity is given to us to bring into play our own faculty for establishing connections – for filling in gaps left by the text itself.

A quotation from a recently published piece of academic literary criticism backs up this point:

> . . . reading can then be seen as a continuous process of forming hypotheses, reinforcing them, developing them, modifying them, and sometimes replacing them by others or dropping them altogether.
>
> (Rimmon-Kenan 1983)

Such a definition of reading is fascinating, coming as it does from a world apparently far removed from that of children developing as readers and even further from the concerns of teachers helping children with reading difficulties. Yet could it be suggested, perhaps, that an approach based on such ideas may well offer a way into reading for all children, and that sessions exploring what is being read in these ways should be considered by special needs teachers? The next two chapters attempt to make a case for just such an approach.

Sally's description of herself in the room, watching Tom, was interesting in that it also gave an indication of the degree of her involvement in the novel. Iser describes such 'involvement' thus: '. . . we actually participate in the text, and this means that we are caught up in the very thing we are producing. That is why we often have the impression, as we read, that we are living another life.'

Attempting to determine the degree of involvement of a reader in a novel is obviously extremely difficult. There appears to be a constant oscillation between 'involvement' and 'detachment', the latter occurring when the reader steps back from the work to consider it. However, from Sally's account, the position of the reader in the scene – where the reader is in the picture he or she forms – seems to be important. Throughout *Tom's Midnight Garden,* Sally was present in the scenes as an observer: 'With Tom I'm looking through something, being able to see him . . . and I'm watching Hattie in the scenes.'

In other novels, though, she remembered her involvement had been rather different:

Sally   In *Little House on the Prairie* I began to feel as if I was actually there with her, as if I was one of the sisters. I think it was Mary, the older one. I was almost there.

Q   Have you ever got there?

S   In *The Lion, the Witch and the Wardrobe* I was Susan and I would never believe Lucy when she told me that she'd gone into another world, and I was there and telling her it wasn't true!

Sally admitted that she preferred to read novels in which she became 'involved' since this involvement was one of the main pleasures to be gained from reading. She felt that in *Tom's Midnight Garden* the fact that the main character, through whose eyes the story takes place, was a boy had prevented her 'becoming a part' of the novel.

The work with Sally demonstrates clearly the subjective element in any reader's appreciation of a fictional work. Her thoughts and feelings, the pictures in her mind and her degree of involvement are all personal. Other readers will no doubt respond differently. The 'significance' of the work for her is due to factors which she brings to her reading – her age, her life experience, her personality, her previous reading of fiction. How these can form the basis for work in the classroom will be explored in the last chapter.

Before that, however, a method of reading with children who have difficulties must be found which enables them to interact with texts in the same way as Sally. The satisfaction she obviously gained from her reading must be experienced by 'poor' readers if they are to be motivated towards books. Recently I listened to another 9-year-old-girl, Jennie, who was also a fluent reader, confident in her ability. She read aloud a passage from *The Animals of Farthing Wood* by Colin Dann. What struck me were two features of her reading. Firstly on a couple of occasions she lost her way in long sentences and began to falter. Each time though she automatically scanned back to the beginning of the sentence and read it again, a note of relief appearing in her voice when she reached the troublesome part and was able to cope with it. Secondly she mispronounced a number of words in such a way as to indicate that she had made no sense of them. But she did not stop. Rather, she carried on, gaining sense from the context. Both of these strategies displayed her confidence but also the fact that her main aim was to make meaning from her reading. She did this automatically as any fluent reader will. But 9-year-olds who are poor readers will not. Some will read on, sentence after sentence, the intonation indicating that they can be making no sense of it, but lacking the confidence and awareness to stop, go back to the beginning and start again. Others will stop at a particular word, not daring to read on until it has been mastered, staring in silence. The automatic strategies of fluent readers have then to be demonstrated to such children. They have to be shown that it is not wrong of them to scan backwards (or forwards) if this helps to make the meaning clear. They have to be shown that we read stories not words. In the next chapter, after some consideration of ways of organizing in schools for these children, a method of approaching reading will be considered which not only provides the support necessary to overcome the tremendous anxiety they feel about reading but allows them to interact with texts in the same way as fluent readers.

CHAPTER 5

Organizing a programme

The experience becomes wretched at present largely because it is a wretched thing to be compelled to do something at which you persistently fail.

(Margaret Donaldson 1978)

In the last chapter the reading of a fluent, keen reader was considered so that attention could be drawn to the attractions of reading and the strategies used by such readers as they make their way through fictional texts. A plea was made for literature to be used as a way into reading for children with reading difficulties in that the power of story is a major driving force in the development of reading in very young children. In Chapter 6 ways of developing children's love of stories and poems and their responses to them will be considered, but before this two other important factors need to be examined. Firstly there is the role and organization of the school. Help for children with reading difficulties, whoever is responsible for it and whatever methods are used, does not take place in a vacuum. The way the work is approached within the school as a whole can make a crucial difference to success or failure. Secondly a method of reading which enables children to have access to 'real' books and to read like 'real' readers has to be found. Struggling with graded texts of stilted prose is unlikely to lead to 'real' reading.

School organization

Work with children who have reading difficulties can become fragmented if there is not a close liaison between those who are trying to help them: parents, class teachers, specialist teachers, and local authority support teams. At the centre of any organization designed to help should be the child, but if the different interested parties are not all working as a team the result can be 'bitty' and fragmented. Before really useful work can be done a school must have a clearly defined policy for helping children such as Leslie.

The policy which evolved at the middle school in which I was working had a number of features, involving both staff and parents. Basically it centred around close co-operation between all of those concerned so that no work was carried out in isolation. The children whose reading gave cause for concern were withdrawn from lessons each day to work with me and I spent a great deal of time discussing with the class teachers work I had done and how they were providing within their classrooms. Whether or not to withdraw children in this way is a contentious issue and I have myself seen it result in a depressing lowering of the children's self-esteem. Groups for the 'thickies' can quickly put an end to any belief in real progress, and without belief there is nothing. To prevent such a state of affairs developing we made sure that these sessions were given status in the children's eyes. It was a privilege to work in Mr Martin's room, and not only a privilege but extremely enjoyable. A great deal of work was done on the children's motivation which is described below and there was a definite assumption which the children had to share that progress would result from the work. They would learn how to read. The second aspect of these withdrawal sessions was equally important – my liaison with the class teachers. Most of this was informal – in the staffroom during breaks or for a few minutes at the beginning and end of each day. However, the important point is that it took place every day and touched on many aspects of the children's life at school. Through it the teachers and I began to increase our awareness of the myriad of facets which contribute towards success or failure with such children. In addition, year group teachers met regularly, such meetings proving extremely useful simply as a chance for everyone to air views, describe successes and admit to problems. The importance of such a 'system' cannot be overstressed: catering for 'special needs' does not mean withdrawal of a child once a week for an hour with a member of the local authority support team, working at something totally unconnected with the classroom work and being left piles of duplicated worksheets to complete in class before the following week's session. Within such a session much good work might well go on, both in the withdrawal sessions and back in class, but where the work goes on in isolation a coherent approach is not established. The child, the thinking child, can become confused and likely to despair. All of these different views of how he should become a reader – which one holds the key?

One further element in this organization is perhaps the most important of all and yet still so often the most neglected: the parents. Involving parents fully in the work wherever possible was a major reason for the success we achieved for two different reasons. These reasons hinged on the fact that some parents were keen and able to help their particular children while others (for a whole variety of reasons) were unable to do so. At the United Kingdom Reading Association conference in Worcester in 1984 Joyce Morris distinguished between 'parent dependent' and 'teacher dependent' children. Most children are parent dependent in that their parents contribute much more than any teacher could to their attitudes and learning. I like to think that my own two children owe more to the way they have grown up in the family than to the effect of school upon them.

However, some children are teacher dependent, in the sense of the school being the major agent of their learning. It seemed to me to be important to determine which parents were going to help at home with the reading and which were unlikely to do so. More of my time could then be spent with those children who were dependent on the school for learning how to read. The others could learn at home - my role being that of guide and counsellor.

The first stage was to write to the parents, inviting them to the school to chat to me about their children. Each letter was hand-written so that it looked informal and, I hoped, none threatening, and simply stated that the parents could come to the school at any time convenient to them. There was no insistence on particular times convenient to the school or me, and there was no need to make an appointment. It was important that I could be available to suit the parents and this usually worked. Within the first few weeks of term I had spoken to someone from the home about each of the children with whom I was going to work. During these initial 'chats' I had one major objective, to ascertain what were the parents' views and feelings about their own particular children not being able to read. If motivation based on self-belief was going to be the major driving force in my work, could the home provide it? Books can be used, workcards completed and games played, but if there is no real determination based on belief that success is eventually possible then there is unlikely to be enough to sustain either parents or children in the long period of time which may well be necessary. It is impossible to generalize about the feelings of parents in this position, but Leslie's mother and father can be used to illustrate certain points. When Leslie first arrived at the middle school he cried a lot, would not try to achieve anything (saying that he could not) and then stayed at home. When returned to school he brought notes about sickness and colds but neither of his parents appeared. Trying to contact them proved extremely difficult and when his mother eventually appeared it became obvious why. She arrived one morning with her sister who had brought her to school because she was too frightened to come up on her own. To gain Leslie's mother's confidence took a long time and many meetings and it was only really gained when Leslie began to make progress - when he began to read. For Leslie's mother too had given up. She did not think her son was ever going to improve. Talk of a place at special school confirmed this in her mind. I can still remember talking to her about the work I was going to do with Leslie and how her head nodded as she listened. But she asked no questions and showed little real interest. She had heard it all before. Changing her views so that her positive belief in Leslie's improvement could act as an impetus to him was a long process. Keeping them both going over the months when nothing seemed to happen was very difficult.

The work I did with Leslie and the other children took place then within a school environment in which all concerned were well aware of the efforts being made. Looking back on this work, three factors seem to have been important without which not nearly as much would have been achieved. All three had to be faced up to by Leslie, involving as they did a realization of his situation and his future. Firstly Leslie had to change the view he had of himself as both a failure and a non-reader. Margaret Donaldson's words at the beginning of this chapter sum up the situation perfectly. Yet even as I read these words again I find I have to force myself into a realization of what they actually meant in Leslie's case. Can we really imagine what it must be like to spend four years in classrooms while all around us friends learn to read and we do not? If as an adult I was going to take up a new hobby or sport, say, badminton, with a group of friends, I would expect over one year (let alone four!) to make some progress. How would I feel if all of my friends developed their skills while I remained totally unable to hit the shuttle over the net? No doubt I would soon give up badminton and try something else. But, of course, children cannot give up school and they should not give up reading when in a literate society print has such power. So day after day, month after month, year after year Leslie came back for more failure. By the age of nine he had given up, seeing himself as a failure at school, someone who was not very clever. While he continued to see himself in this light, progress would be extremely difficult.

Connected with this general failure was the view Leslie had of himself as a reader. Children (and adults) who see themselves as readers react to the print environment, its books, posters, signs, headings, labels. They expect to be able to read them. Leslie did not. Consequently he did not think that this environment was for him and took little notice of it. A 5-year-old, confident in his developing ability, will ask if he is unable to read something. For Leslie to ask was yet another admission of failure. So he kept quiet, ignoring the print which surrounded him. If he was to become a reader he first of all had to see himself as one.

The second major factor was the need for Leslie to realize that the way ahead was likely to be long and difficult. Instant results were not expected. This applied as much to Leslie's parents as to Leslie for they had experienced his failure with him and like him had despaired. However, there had, thirdly, to be a belief that the work really was going to lead him to reading. I wonder how many teachers genuinely believe that the non-readers they are working with will actually become fluent readers? Yet just such a belief must underpin the work. If I did not believe it, why should Leslie? This is easy to write now, after the event, but it would be wrong of me not to refer to the constant see-sawing between belief and doubt, hope and despair, that was a feature of the work. Some days for no apparent reason Leslie would do so well and I would feel we really were on the verge of a breakthrough. Then, just as inexplicably, he would struggle so badly that it was as if nothing had been achieved by all the hard work. There were times when I felt almost total despair, desperately searching for something, anything, to move him a little further along the path. Nothing seemed to work. We were wasting our time.

The above principles underlined the work which was done both in the withdrawal lessons and back in the classroom. I must stress again how necessary it was for all those who were working with Leslie and the others to have agreed to them. In addition we had to make a commitment to providing enough time to give the sort of help we felt was so necessary, which resulted in Leslie reading with me on almost every school day for three years. Some schools have argued that such time cannot be provided – too many other things need to be done. It is difficult to disagree with such arguments except to say that if only infrequent, short periods of help are available then there is unlikely to be much progress. And with children such as Leslie time is running out. Within a 9–13 middle school the four years were looked upon as being the time we had to turn Leslie into a reader. To Leslie four years might seem an eternity (hence the necessity of making him realize that a solution to his problem would not be instant). But in fact four years was a very short period of time in which to overcome the accumulated reading failure of his life so far. The involvement of parents wherever possible has already been mentioned and help at home really does take the pressure off teachers faced with problems of time. In my last year at the school (84/85) I extended this involvement by organizing two volunteer parents to help the children who were not receiving much help at home. They were told that the work would entail them coming up to school on each and every school day for an hour. Each of them was to help three particular children. Twenty minutes each day for each child. These parents responded magnificently, trudging up to school in all weathers. They built up excellent relationships with the children and by the end of the year were excited by the progress some of the children were making. What could not be denied was the effect on the children concerned in terms of their general confidence in school. And without confidence, there would have been no progress.

As well as a commitment within the school to time for the children who needed help, the class teachers also had an important role to play in terms of how they provided in class. Leslie and the others spent much of each school day in mixed-ability classrooms. There were four important aspects of their work which contributed towards the progress made by the children. The first was their ability to inspire confidence in the children; to motivate them so that they believed in themselves. A lot of this was obviously down to the individual teacher's personality and the quality of the relationships that were established. But of equal importance was the second aspect of their work – the extent to which they involved the children in the everyday classwork and made them feel a part of the class. In Chapter 2 attention was drawn to the problem of these children seeing themselves as different, especially if they are withdrawn for extra help. We found that when they arrived at the middle school some assumed that the work in class was not for them. Confidence and motivation would come from being fully involved. Success with such a strategy was dependent on a third factor: the quality of the relationship between the teacher and the other children in the class – those who did not 'go to Mr Martin'. There was a need for a supportive environment to be created. An atmosphere in which help could be requested without fear of rejection or ridicule, and everyone was aware of the problems faced by some of their classmates. So a teacher might spend time talking to her class about the difficulties of someone like Leslie; engaging their sympathy and enlisting their help. Praise from another member of the class proved to be worth a very great deal. Finally the class teachers had to be willing to liaise constantly with me about the work we were doing. I had to know what Leslie was doing in class so that I was working in unison with his teacher. One result of this was that work could be brought from class to the withdrawal sessions and part of our time spent working on it.

A reading method

The importance of the organization we tried to establish within the school cannot be overstressed. Work was going on within an environment where all interested parties were heading in the same direction. Leslie and the others were getting help from a number of teachers (not only in the ways described above – some teachers offered to work during their lunch hours in order to provide the time which we felt was so desperately important), their parents wherever possible, volunteer parents at school and their peers in the classroom. As the work progressed so ideas changed; strategies where tried and then either incorporated into the programme or rejected. As I became more and more convinced of the necessity of using 'real' books and a method which enabled the children to read like 'real' readers, unconcious of the words and responding to the ideas, much of what we had begun with was abandoned. For instance the games we had played were extremely popular. 'Hunt and Stab' was constantly requested in the early days, the children having to search from a pile of cards for words which I would call out, stabbing the particular card with a finger. But such a game drew attention to just that surface quality of print – words – with which the children were obsessed. Search for words in a game and the danger is that you think that is what reading is all about. This displayed itself early on when I first allowed the children to choose freely, from within the selection available, the books they wished to read. Leslie's record cards (quoted in Chapter 1) displayed clearly that he had got 'stuck' on particular reading schemes and, as he had failed to make progress, been 'helped' by extra work on phonics, word building and word recognition. For him to have been presented with yet another numbered reading scheme would simply have compounded his feelings of failure. But as he and the others searched for a book to read, it became clear that the major priority was not the quality of the book, the subject matter which might have been of interest, but whether or not they would be able to get the words right when they read it. For them, reading meant reading aloud. They were the ones who always read to the teacher and in this situation, which they most definitely saw as a test of their ability, reading meant getting the words right. And is that not what teachers mean when they say to a child who has just read to them, 'well read'? Surely 'well read' must mean that you got the words right. So in choosing a book this will be the most important criterion.

In addition to altering their attitude to the books they were going to read I also believed it was necessary to alter their perceptions of the print environment in which they were living. I have mentioned earlier the lack of reaction of these 9-year-olds to the print around them and well remember the morning we went on a 'tour' of the school to look at 'school print'. Knowing their problems I had expected difficulties with the notice boards, directions and signs around the school but to watch the group trying to make sense of them was quite a shock. Such written material as messages from teachers concerning sporting events and practices might as well have been written in Chinese! The children admitted never having tried to read these before, normally gleaning the meaning from listening to friends. So a crucial way in which vocabulary can be developed was ignored. This seems to be connected with problems of vocabulary they encountered in their reading. Time and again it was the lack of understanding of a particular word which meant that the comprehension of a sentence or even a paragraph was affected. They did not know the meaning of many, many words which other children of their age understood. Two reasons appeared to have caused this: firstly the way they had switched off their reactions to the print environment around them at school, at home and in the street; secondly four years of only reading simplified material from which so much language is excluded. The tragedy is that by the age of 9 so much has been missed.

The reading programme which developed was then designed to provide three complementary experiences: times when a child would read to an adult in such a way that it could not be seen as a test, the aim being to get behind the words to the story and the ideas; times for silent reading and browsing through books; and lastly a conscious attempt to use the print environment. At about the time when I was beginning to wonder what sort of reading session would allow us to achieve our objectives, *Dyslexia or Illiteracy* (1983) by Young and Tyre was drawn to my attention. In this book they describe a form of paired reading which they developed for use with children who had reading difficulties. Some of these children had been classified as 'dyslexic', others as slow or backward readers, and their research indicated very encouraging results with both groups. While willing to try anything that appeared to 'work', the method also attracted me because it seemed to offer just that experience of reading I wanted the children to have.

It can be summarized as follows:

1   Adult reads aloud to the child for a few minutes. This is a dramatic reading with much emphasis on intonation.
2   Adult and child re-read the same piece of text together. The adult is very much the leader, and the child tries to join in as well as imitating the intonation.
3   The child takes the lead in a further re-reading with the adult.
4   The child reads the text un-aided.

Before looking at what turned out to be the attractions of this method, one very important point must be made. In no way must it be allowed to become a rigid exercise. Exactly what happens at each reading session will depend on the adult, the child and the book. Sometimes I read all of the time, at others the child might take more of the responsibility. Sometimes we spent a lot of time just talking about what we were reading. In the next chapter I focus on this 'sharing' of books between reader and non-reader; at this point I just want to ensure that flexibility is seen as the key to success. This method of reading with the children offers a range of attractions all of which become apparent as I made use of it:

1 Support is given to the struggling child from the start. Leslie indicates in Chapter 1 how frightened and 'embarrassed' he was at reading aloud (especially to the headmistress), and all of the children were under great pressure not to get 'stuck on a word'. This fear dominated their attitude towards reading and had to be removed before progress could begin to be made. Karl, mentioned in Chapter 2, demonstrated this panic more vividly than any of the others. For him reading aloud was a terrifying experience. Within a few seconds of 'getting stuck' the eyes would start wandering all over the place, desperate for clues. The feet would tap, the head shake, the hands twitch. It took him two years to admit to such feelings, and only when he was able to face up to them and describe how the words just 'jumped about' and he came out in a cold sweat did he begin to make progress. Quite by coincidence in September 1982 when I began working with the group I was given a piano. A long-held dream of mine had been to learn the piano but I had never had a music lesson in my life. Nevertheless I found a sympathetic music teacher, bought Book 1 of the course and began. Now I was confident and learning voluntarily but some of those lessons were purgatory! Pieces of music which I could play at home, relaxed and alone, suddenly became impossible. Something seemed to block the message held in the printed notes and my hands would freeze. I would find myself soaked in sweat and very frustrated. The mere fact of having the teacher watch me created tensions which impaired my playing. Like Karl, the print 'jumped about' and made no sense (could I be a dyslexic piano player I wondered?). It seemed that much the same was happening to me as was happening to those children – except of course that I was free to continue or give up. Playing the piano is nowhere near as important as learning to read. With the above approach to reading, getting stuck on words does not occur in the early stages when confidence is being built up. As the children began to relax and make progress we modified our use of the method so that moments were allowed for them to think about the words and have a go before they were supplied.

2 This approach ensures that the meaning of the passage is established first, the children's attention being focused on the ideas behind the words rather than the words themselves. As they gradually take over the reading of a passage the fact that they already know what is happening provides the support necessary for them to read the words. This means that they are reading like fluent readers from the start, concious of the meaning and using the words to create that meaning.

3   During a reading session the child comes into contact with a lot of print. The problem with using specially written texts for 'remedial readers' which the child reads slowly aloud is that at the end of a session he has not actually read many words. But in order to make that leap from struggling with graded texts to reading fluently he must literally do a lot of reading. In a twenty-minute session with, say, *The Iron Man* the child really does read a lot of words. And of course the vast majority are the same words which appear in any text repeated over and over again. It is only through reading that the child will learn to read.

4   Following from the last point is the way in which this approach provides a way for the child to develop an awareness of the rhythms of written language. Margaret Clark in *Young Fluent Readers* (1976) drew attention to the way in which pre-school children listening to stories being read aloud build up an appreciation of how written language sounds. Such an appreciation enables them to find their way through a text when they are reading. Again, 'reading books' often lack these rhythms, the text being too simple. In addition the aim of the writers of these books is often to provide particular types of texts (for instance texts which draw attention to particular phonic patterns) which can result in either a total lack of any rhythmic style or in the worst cases a stilted robotic style which is not going to help any child develop reading fluency.

5   Because the child is reading with a fluent reader he is presented with a model of how such readers read texts. This is especially important in terms of intonation patterns for the child to imitate. When adult and child read together the child tries to read in the same way as the adult with the same intonation. In addition great use can be made of varying the pace of the reading depending on what is happening and of drawing attention to pauses. This means that the adult reading really must be 'dramatic'. It is through intonation, pace and pauses that we come to an appreciation of what the passage is all about. Once the children relaxed (and because my readings were always 'over the top'!) this feature of the work became a great attraction.

6   The fact that this approach allows one to use 'real' books written by 'real' authors has been mentioned in terms of a number of the above points. It also means that use is made of books that are worth reading! Children come to stories early on in their lives and the magic is due to the way such stories excite, frighten, make one laugh and cry. Just think of the popular folk and fairy tales and the wide-eyed look on a young child's face when Sleeping Beauty pricks her finger on the spindle and falls asleep. If children who have failed to learn to read are to be motivated, a great deal of that motivation must come from a growing realization that books are worth reading. You cannot tell them that. Until a child experiences a book which really moves him in some way, catching him up in its action, he cannot know what the world of books has to offer. If such powerful books can actually be read by the child with the support this approach offers, so that at the end of a session he

really wants to know what is going to happen next, motivation is provided from reading itself. External inducements become redundant. The child wants to read the book because of what the book itself has to offer.

7 The approach can easily be adopted by all those helping the children concerned. I found that it was best to actually demonstrate it to individual parents who were invited up to school. When they saw the way in which it worked with their own children they felt confident in taking it home and making it the basis of their help.

The above points make, I believe, an extremely strong case for the use of this variation of paired reading with children who have experienced difficulty learning to read. When I first considered it my one doubt was that it might prove somewhat boring for the children in that the same piece of text would be read four times. However, this was most certainly not the case. I had not appreciated fully the tremendous thrill the children got from being able to read pages of novels with very little help, even if it was the fourth reading. I had not realized the great satisfaction this gave them. I had not seen the situation from their perspective.

Apart from the sessions when we read together and talked about the books, I believed it was important to encourage the children to read silently. Reading is, naturally, a silent activity and we only ever read aloud on rare occasions. In addition, whenever we do have to read aloud we feel under pressure no matter how fluent and confident we might be. Just as I could play the piano better when I was alone, so these children needed to be alone with books. Sometimes this meant sessions just browsing through books quietly in the classroom. A collection of reference books, picture books, story books and poetry anthologies is all that is required. The children were allowed time to choose, browse, choose again, share things of interest, read silently. After one such session we talked about the difference between reading aloud and reading silently (what the children called 'reading in your mind'). All of them felt that they read better to themselves than to another person. They felt that they could 'get into the book'. They spoke about 'getting stuck' and 'nobody knows'. On their own they could 'do lots of things' to make their way through the print and mentioned specifically 'trying to work it out', 'looking at the picture', and 'missing it out'. They were encouraged to have books at home, by their beds, and to read quietly each evening. It was explained to the parents that this was as important as the reading sessions with them. It seems to me to be essential that from a very early age children are left alone with books.

This discussion of the merits of silent reading assumes, of course, a particular ability on the part of the reader and the provision of suitable reading materials. Whereas the method of paired reading described above allows for support and help, silent reading means having to make one's way through the book alone. Too many words missed out and reading really does become a 'guessing game' with very little sense made of what is read. This was a problem that faced us throughout our work and was never really solved satisfactorily. Books which could be managed alone were either written for younger children or were part of the 'remedial' material. The subject matter of the former was not suitable for 10-year-olds who very definitely wanted 'grown up' looking books, while the problems associated with the latter have been discussed above. Their language frequently defied intonation and had been so pared down and simplified that only the words remained. No rhythm of language or the sort of redundancy of language which helps us all when we read. There is an enormous gulf between the most 'difficult' graded readers and the world of children's literature. Nevertheless we browsed through picture books (many on the market appeal to older children), reference books, a selection of books from different schemes and stories they had read aloud with help. They enjoyed taking home books already read to read alone, knowing that they could make their way through them successfully. But the search for suitable material for reading silently was never ending.

In this chapter two aspects of work have been considered. Firstly there is the need for a whole school organization if the needs of these children are to be in any real way catered for: a common approach offered by all of those concerned. Secondly a method of approaching reading with children who have difficulties has been advocated. This form of paired reading has many merits, but basically it allows the children to read like 'real' readers, providing the necessary model and support for them to do so. Now the world of literature is open to them and we need to consider how to harness this world in order that its power can be appreciated by those who have been excluded from it.

CHAPTER 6

Readers and books: literature for the failures

Readers are made when they discover the activity is 'worth it'. Poor inadequate, inexperienced readers lack literary competence because they have too little idea of what is 'in' reading for them.'

(Margaret Meek 1983)

The above quotation lies at the heart of what I am proposing in this book. The variation of paired reading described in the last chapter allows us to offer the world of literature to struggling readers and in so doing enables them to experience its power. If they are to become readers they must discover what is in literature for them. Margaret Meek has argued elsewhere (*Achieving Literacy*) that the best teachers of reading may well be the authors of the books children read. It is only by making one's way through a variety of novels that one can begin to appreciate how novels work; one develops 'literary competence' through reading. Sally demostrated just such competence in Chapter 4. However, there is much interesting work which can, and should go on in classrooms to help children develop as readers; work based on an awareness of the reading process. In the introduction I argued that such ideas do not appear in books about children with reading difficulties. Hence teachers whose major interest lies in this field are often unaware of them. The work of contemporary literary critics is beginning to find its way into books and articles aimed at teachers in both primary and secondary schools (see the suggestions for further reading), but it does not appear to be seen as relevant to the children we are concerned with in this book. In this chapter I want to consider the factors which influence a reader's response to a work of literature and suggest practical ways of developing 'literary competence'. Failing readers must get involved in the world of books and experience the power of story and imaginative language. If they remain outside this world a major motivation for learning to read is denied them.

In Chapter 4 the way in which a 9-year-old girl, Sally, read the novel *Tom's Midnight Garden* was examined. Sally demonstrated how the significance a novel has for a particular reader is to a large extent subjective, dependent on what the reader brings to the reading of the work. Different readers might all understand the words on the page but the significance of those words for each reader will depend upon other factors. As Iser (1978) puts it:

> The significance of the work, then, does not lie in the meaning sealed within the text, but in the fact that this meaning brings out what had previously been sealed within us.

Now what areas of prior experience does a reader bring to a literary work? Firstly all that reader's previous life experience! As Fred Inglis (1981) points out:

> We respond (to the characters) in complex ways, to and for them out of the framework of all our prior experiences.

To give an obvious example, I could not respond to Robert Graves' novel *Goodbye to All That* in the same way as someone who had fought in the First World War. To have experienced the subject matter of the novel will greatly influence the 'significance' that novel has for a reader. In that novels are about people, we can all recognize and respond to the characters, but here again the past-life experience of the reader must play a major part. Our experience of people and our relationships with them will to a large extent determine our reactions. I had the unfortunate experience of being educated at a boarding school. Give me a novel set in a boarding school and, no matter how detailed the description, I am back in the dormitories I knew! The psychoanalytic critic, Simon Lesser (1957), goes further and describes how readers seek analogies from their own lives in order to comprehend fiction:

> In addition to participating vicariously in the stories in which we become absorbed, we frequently create and imaginitively act out stories structured upon them. We analogize. The stories we spin are, of course, highly elliptical. There is neither time nor need to develop them systematically. Analogizing may involve nothing more than the recognition of a similarity between a fictional event and something which has happened to us, and a rapid reliving of the experience . . . Analogizing . . . is so closely akin to daydreaming.

Examples of children involved in just such a process were obtained when I worked with Sally, she being one of a trio of children who talked on tape with me about their reading. Points of comparison were often made between their own lives and those of the characters in the novels. For instance Helen (aged 12) on 'mother' in Nina Bawden's *The Peppermint Pig*:

> I thought of my mum . . . she's always telling me off . . . but it's good for me really.

Gavin (aged 9) was drawn towards Tom in *Tom's Midnight Garden* as a fellow-sufferer at the hands of 'loving' adults!

> He doesn't like his Aunt Gwen because she's a child lover and he don't like people

like them. He don't like people who go on at you and things like and that and bothering too much about you, saying you can't do things you want.

The fact that a reader's previous life experience will influence the way in which that reader responds to a novel means that a great opportunity is created for teachers and children to share responses to books read. By asking such questions as 'Does anything in the story remind you of things which have happened to you or ways you have felt?' discussion can be initiated in which both teacher and child have equal status in terms of their readings. Neither response can be said to be 'correct'. Both are valid if the story touched off connections with real-life situations. This can result in a great raising of the attitudes and feelings of child readers, especially those who have struggled with reading. Suddenly stories in books are seen to have relevance to their own lives, and, equally important, these connections are accepted and valued by other readers. No longer is the aim of reading to 'get it right'. Instead an exploration of literature in terms of the effects it has on us begins to be put into motion.

Of course the above approach means that teachers can no longer see themselves as the possessors of correct interpretations of works of literature. Questions such as 'What does that word/sentence/paragraph mean?' would not appear to offer much in terms of exploring a story. They could be used to focus on the meanings of particular words that might require explanation, but this should not take up more than a minimum of time. It is the thoughts, ideas and feelings which the words create in the reader's mind which should be the basis for a lot of the work. As adults, of course, our life experience will mean that we are going to see events in stories from an adult perspective. We must be very careful not to assume that our perspective is correct, and (however unintentionally) force it onto children. As Nina Bawden (1976) has written:

And their view is necessarily limited. They cannot understand, for example, the desperate anxiety, the helpless love, that adults feel for them.

Her own novel *The Peppermint Pig* contains a good example of this, as it recounts the problems of a mother bringing up a family on her own:

She (i.e. mother) gave a long sigh, looking into the fire, and then her face twisted suddenly and she turned to Lily and said, almost desperately, 'Remember, Lily, that's the worst thing about poverty! Not hunger or leaky boots but the way it drains your spirit! However things turn out, you must never let that happen to you. Promise me!' Poll said, bewildered, 'I would hate to be hungry,' and her mother gasped and jumped up from the chair and put her arms around her, holding her so close and tight that Poll could hear her heart fluttering.

'Oh my lamb, of course you're never going to be. Did I frighten you? That was stupid, there's nothing to be frightened of. Everything is going to be all right, you must believe me'.

As a parent myself, this scene and others like it had a real significance for me. I could analogize about my own children and feel how Poll's mother felt. But whenever I have talked about it with young readers, it has become obvious that they do not read the scene in the same way as I do. They see what is happening through Poll's eyes rather than her mother's, and of course have not had the experience to be able to appreciate what I feel and, presumably, what Nina Bawden felt. While I can share my feelings with them, explaining as best I can what significance the scene has for me, I must also accept the way they react to it.

A second, connected factor which we bring to novels and which will determine what significance we find in them is concerned with our psychological make-up. We bring our characteristic psychological traits. Critic Norman Holland (1980) describes what happens thus:

> . . . we interpret the new experience in such a way as to cast it in the terms of our characteristic ways of coping with the world. That is, each of us will find in the literary work the kind of thing we characteristically wish or fear the most. Therefore, to respond, we need to be able to re-create from the literary work our characteristic strategies for dealing with those deep fears and wishes.

With regard to children, Nicholas Tucker (1981) draws attention to their responses to fiction in terms of their psychological development. He argues for a child's need to feel secure in reading, mentioning the short repetitive plots of both traditional folk tales and Enid Blyton. The popularity of both is due, to a large extent, to children knowing in advance that any disturbing action will be resolved in the end. (The same features no doubt account for the popularity of such mass-produced adult fiction as that published by Mills and Boon.) Helen, having read *The Peppermint Pig,* talked about the ending and her reactions to Poll's father coming back after a year in America:

> It was like something happening in real life though I don't think it would happen *just* like that in real life. I think something would have happened to their father . . . it was too happy in the end . . . I don't like stories with happy endings, well I do but sometimes I think they ought to have tragic endings

Helen seems torn between a desire for happy endings and the security they bring, and her realization that they are not in fact realistic.

The work of Piaget is relevant here in two ways. Firstly, he has demonstrated how children's cognitive development shows a progession from thinking in very concrete terms to abstract thought. Until children have developed the ability to think abstractly, they will be far more concerned with action and dialogue than with passages of description or introspection.

Gavin read the final hundred pages of *Tom's Midnight Garden* in two evenings and, when asked about them, gave a description of a series of scenes:

> Well, Tom goes into the garden and he meets Hattie – and nobody could see him except Hattie and the gardener – they build a tree house and Hattie falls out and she has to go into her room. So Tom went in and had a talk and then came back out again and the next time he went back in she was in her teens and she was skating and

Tom asked her to put some skates in a secret place which only Tom and her knew about and she did and Tom found them – and they skated on the river and got picked up and went back and next day, next night, the garden wasn't there, it was just the old yard it had always been – and next day he went to Mrs Bartholomew's house and she had left skates and things and skated all the way to Ely and Peter, Tom's brother, had been with them at Ely and when they got back Peter faded away and when he asked Mrs Bartholomew all about it she knew all about it.

Now, an adult, experienced reader, on being asked about the end of *Tom's Midnight Garden* would almost certainly comment on the fact that the meaning of the novel is made plain during a long conversation between Tom and Mrs Bartholomew. Indeed, Sally, an experienced child reader, did just this as we saw in Chapter 4: 'Well I've found out that Mrs Bartholomew was Hattie and she had been dreaming of when she was young . . .'

Gavin, although a fluent reader, was nowhere near as experienced a reader as Sally. Neither was he such an avid reader. His response to the novel was in terms of its action, and his interest in its 'meaning' had not been aroused. He had obviously skimmed over the conversation between Tom and Mrs Bartholomew:

Q And why was the garden there, appearing each night?
Gavin I don't know – it didn't tell me.
Q Why does Tom get thinner and thinner?
G I don't know really.

When the relevant extract was read aloud to Gavin, he was able to understand it and answer the questions correctly. So it appears that his lack of awareness was due to a lack of interest in the scene. Nothing much happened. Indeed when I asked him to close his eyes, think about the book and give his thoughts, he said: 'I see a tree falling down when the lightning strikes it'. A very dramatic scene is what remains in Gavin's memory.

In terms of working with children who are extremely inexperienced readers, i.e. children who have failed to learn to read, we can learn something from Gavin. The search needs to be made for novels and stories in which the action rattles along, carrying the reader with it. In this way the basic structure of story can be used by the reader and interest be maintained. A great resource here is the wealth of folk and fairy tales from around the world, tales which have lasted precisely because they have both power and action. The combination of archetypal human themes with fast-moving action makes them very powerful stories for the classroom. Both children and adults find them difficult to resist. In addition many contain elements which repeat, almost ritualistically, which can be used by the reader as another prop for making his way through them. There have always been anthologies of such tales on the market but recently some really beautiful editions have appeared (see booklist on page 83). Edna O'Brien's *Tales for the Telling: Irish Folk and Fairy Stories*, illustrated by Michael Forman, is an excellent example. In this collection the language is rich and yet simple in the best traditions of good story telling. Look at the opening of 'The Fool':

> There once was a king in the western part of Ireland and he had a son that was called Amada. Amada's mother died and the king married again but the stepmother didn't like the son and she never gave him anything tasty to eat. She fed him on meal and water, and nettles. However, he did grow up to be strong and the stepmother was afraid that he would harm her own children so she asked her husband, the king, to send him away but Amada refused to go until his father would give him a sword that was so sharp it would cut a fleck of wool falling on it. The king knew a famous blacksmith, who was in debt to him, and he asked him to make a sword that had no equal in the land and they called this sword the 'Invincible'.

Surely this sort of text contains all the elements we would wish for children who have struggled with reading.

Folk and fairy tales, with their wicked stepmothers, brave princes and frightening giants, possess another feature which makes them so accessible to children. Piaget's studies of the moral development of children suggest that they tend to see people as either 'good' or 'bad' and the world as an ordered place in which 'good' will ultimately triumph and 'evil' fail. Many children may then find it difficult to respond to characters who are three-dimensional, 'real' people. They will try to fit them into a clearly demarcated category. I have certainly found this to be so with children. For instance, two girls (Helen and Michelle) seemed unable to comprehend fully many of the attitudes expressed in *The Peppermint Pig*. One good example of this was their attitude to Mrs Marigold Bug, a childhood friend of the mother who appears one day when the children are out walking with their Aunt Harriet:

> Aunt Harriet said, 'This is Mrs Bug, children. She and your mother were dressmaking apprentices together.
> Mrs Bug weaved her head backwards and forwards. Poll thought – not a caterpillar, a snake! A snake that is going to strike! The snake hissed, 'Poor little fatherless things!'

The children are very upset at how rude and cruel Marigold Bug is concerning their father's leaving for America (. . . but I suppose blood will out,') but both Aunt Harriet and Poll's mother try to excuse her because she has led such a hard life, ('. . . husband and two babies dead of consumption, only Noah left now').

An adult reader will appreciate Aunt Harriet's words but the two child readers remained as unconcerned with the excuses as are the child characters in the novel. To them she remained something nasty and physically repulsive. Helen, asked why Poll's mother did not want them to be rude to Mrs Bug, replied: 'She doesn't want to give them a bad reputation.' She answered as a child who had obviously been told that it was impolite to be rude to adults. She saw the action from the viewpoint of her own experience.

I am certainly not suggesting that children should only read fiction in which the characters are clearly black or white. I believe that we can learn much about both other people and ourselves through reading. Confident, fluent readers should be encouraged to try more demanding works. But the children we are concerned with in this book are neither fluent nor confident and I believe that the raw power of an age-old folk tale is more likely to draw them into the world of reading. 'Certainly the success of Ted Hughes' *The Iron Man* with such children is due to its connections with the old tales.

Finally we must consider the way in which readers bring with them an appreciation of the formal characteristics of texts, based on previous reading, which in turn affects the way new texts are appreciated. Consider what is meant by a reader who says on finishing a novel, 'I liked the way it was written.' Whether the satisfaction is felt with the language used, the neatness of the plot, the clever resolution of conflicts, the way the author has made use of chapters, or the images evoked by the text, what are being referred to are the formal characteristics of the work. We have referred already to the alternation between involvement in and detachment from a story as we read it, when Sally's reading of *Tom's Midnight Garden* was examined in Chapter 4. It is when a reader is involved with the work that he is unlikely to be consciously aware of how the formal characteristics of the work are affecting him. The author may have very consciously decided on particular literary strategies to affect the reader but the reader may not be aware of them. However, at times when the reader separates himself from the work and consciously considers it, he may come to realize how response has been due to these formal properties of style and structure. And the more, and wider, one reads, the more one builds up an awareness of how novels and stories work. As the critic Jonathan Culler (1980) states:

> It is clear that the study of one poem or novel facilitates the study of the next: one gains not only points of comparison but a sense of how to read.

Could it be suggested that the use of graded texts for children with reading difficulties – a very narrow diet – might actually prevent them developing this awareness? A similar argument can, I believe, be used to question most of the reading schemes to be found in classrooms across the country.

The children who were interviewed illustrated these points. Firstly there was Helen considering the end of *The Peppermint Pig*, which concludes with Poll's father arriving home after a year's absence. Poll has had a pet pig (Johnnie) for much of this time, but now it has been slaughtered for meat:

> Doors closed. Silence, except for the creep and hiss of the fire and small, squeaky sounds as Mac dreamed in his basket. Father lifted her head away from his shoulder and said, 'Well, what's been happening to you!'
> She tried to think. So much – but she could only remember one thing. A little pig, sitting in a pint beer mug and squealing. A bigger pig, trotting behind mother when she went shopping. A naughty pig, the talk of the town, sitting good as gold in the drawing room of the Manor House with his head in his hostess's lap. A portly pig, snoozing on the doorstep in the sun ...
> Johnnie the peppermint pig, gone now like this whole long year of her *life*, but fixed and safe in her mind, for ever and ever.
> She said 'Johnnie's dead.'
> Father looked at her, puzzled, but smiling. He cupped her chin in his hand and said 'My darling, who's Johnnie?'

These are the closing words of the novel, and talking to Helen it was obvious that they had greatly affected her:

> It was like something happening in real life though I don't think it would happen *just* like that in real life. I think something would have happened to their father . . . it was too happy in the end . . . I don't like stories with happy endings, well I do but sometimes I think they ought to have tragic endings. But it wouldn't be so good in this case because it was a good last line when the father asked who Johnnie was.

Helen's final comment displays clearly her awareness of the novel as an author's creation with its own characteristics. She likes the ending Nina Bawden has chosen and realizes that the need for such an ending might outweigh purely 'realistic' criteria. The novel is an 'artificial' creation and such an 'artificial' ending completes it as a piece of art. Her views are those of a girl who has already read widely and who is bringing her reading experience to bear on this novel. No doubt included in this experience will be other skills: awareness of allusions, of clues, of metaphorical devices for example. And such awarenesses will almost certainly be unconcious. The more novels read, and the greater the variety in terms of subject matter, style and structure, the more the reader is likely to become aware of how novels work.

Michelle was asked about Poll catching scarlet fever (an episode which follows the death of a young child from the same disease and which causes Poll's family to fear for her life):

Q   Did you think she might die?
Michelle Well she might have but I didn't think she would. Most of the time they don't.
Q   What do you mean?
M   Well in books they don't usually die half-way through.

Michelle has realized that heroes and heroines in novels do not normally die in the middle of the story (at least in her reading experience; she appears to be in for a bit of a shock when she comes across *Wuthering Heights!*). Perhaps Michelle's reactions to Poll's illness would have been different if this had been the first novel she had ever read.

A reading of a story or novel will then be a very personal affair. While the text will provide the parameters within which a reader can respond, that response will vary from reader to reader. No two readers could read the same novel in exactly the same way. And it is just this interaction between reader and text which accounts for the power of literature. Reading is a dynamic process in which the reader contributes as much as (more than?) the author. Children who have developed the reading habit know all about this (though of course they may not be able to put it into words), but children who have never been 'caught up' in a novel must find the whole business of reading at school both puzzling and frustrating. Children who are still struggling to master reading are highly unlikely to be aware of what reading could hold for them. This book argues that the form of paired reading described earlier enables such children to experience the power of literature, and that through such experience they can learn to read.

The aim of the above (together with the chapter on Sally's reading of *Tom's Midnight Garden*) has been to bring to the attention of teachers some of the ideas concerning reader-response and the reading process which are now finding their way into 'literature' lessons in both primary and secondary schools. Books such as *Developing Response to Fiction* by Robert Protherough and *Teaching Literature 9–14* by Benton and Fox go into this area in much more depth, offering fascinating insights into how readers respond to literature and how best teachers can help children develop as readers. My contention is that teachers who are not particularly interested in this work will miss such books, and this applies to teachers concerned about children with reading difficulties. Yet I am convinced that an approach through story and literature is not only a necessary antidote to the skills-based approach so often advocated for such children, but is a powerful alternative. Firstly 'narrative' is now becoming recognized as a fundamental way in which human beings organize experience. As the literary critic Wayne Booth (1983) states:

> We are the stories we tell and could tell.

We think in narrative, fantasize in narrative, see our lives and the lives of others in narrative terms. Members of any small group of people meeting will relate anecdotes, whether to establish themselves within the group or, on a more formal level, to back up arguments and opinions. Secondly when this basic human characteristic is developed in imaginative stories and novels something immensely powerful is created, as the quotations in the above section indicate. At the classroom level, any infant teacher can testify to the wide-eyed, open-mouthed look on young children's faces when a story is read aloud. The intensity created at such times is unique to story sessions. Surely we must harness this power in our work with children who cannot read.

I would argue then that the power of imaginative literature should be seen as a way into reading for children who have struggled to learn to read and the paired reading approach described in the last chapter means that children who are not yet independent readers can read it and respond to it like 'real' readers. They will be able to bring themselves to the reading in the ways outlined above. How then, apart from reading the pages with the child, can the teacher share this reading in ways which will enable the child to enter the world of books and be motivated towards reading? Before considering novels and poetry separately, a general point can be made regarding them both. This is quite simple and yet is also perhaps the most neglected factor: teachers should be both knowledgeable and enthusiastic about the world of children's literature. It sounds so obvious and yet it has to be said that in my experience far too many teachers know little about the books the children in their classes are reading. And it is difficult to be enthusiastic about something you know little about. It is impossible to share something that you do not possess. But enthusiasm lies at the heart of all really successful teaching, and we can all remember someone who because of their enthusiasm fired us with the desire to become involved in a subject at school or a hobby at home. Each generation passes on its enthusiasm to the next: hence the millions who go fishing at weekends for example. Television has realized this, and who could fail to be interested in natural history when David Attenborough wades out into a jungle swamp? We can feel the passionate interest of Michael Wood as he searches for the battlefields of the Dark Ages. The teacher who is able to 'chat' enthusiastically about a novel or a poem being read by a child, who can refer to the 'good bits', will be raising the status of reading in the child's eyes. In addition the child will enjoy this sharing and want to develop it, and will be far more likely to take advice about further reading from such a teacher. If we want children to become readers – especially if we want children who have experienced years of failure to put all of that behind them and look to the future – we must infect them with our own enthusiasm.

My own talks to teachers about the world of children's books are geared towards sharing my enthusiasm with them in the hope that some of it will rub off. The basic problem that raises its head is time, in that many teachers imply by their comments that they have no time to keep up with the stream of books now available for children. Underlying such comments, though rarely stated, is a rationale for the use of reading schemes. Books on a reading scheme for beginners become known as child after child uses them, and I am sure few teachers actually read the books which make up the junior end of the reading scheme market (unless they suffer from insomnia!). A child can be moved through from Book 1 to Book 97 without the teacher having to read them, because the decisions regarding which books that child should read are taken by the scheme itself. Is it too unreasonable to argue that the use of reading schemes actually results in some teachers staying ignorant of children's books? And yet there are ways of finding out what is going on, and time can (and must) be found for the reading. With regard to 'finding out', there are now a number of journals and other publications which appear throughout the year containing both articles and reviews (see booklist at the end of the book). Many schools do in fact subscribe to these and many more make use of the expertise on offer from their local library service.

With regard to the time for reading, a simple solution is to be found if schools and teachers provide time for children to read silently or (with younger ones) to browse and share books together. In the last chapter I argued for the need to give children the time to be alone with books in a calm, quiet atmosphere. Given a choice of reading matter even poor and/or reluctant readers will sit with books. The children I worked with always reckoned they could read better 'in their minds'. Indeed Leslie referred to his younger brother who also had 'trouble with his reading' and the fact that the teacher always heard him read more than the other children. Of course the teacher's aim was to provide extra help – I have heard many teachers argue that they make time for the poor readers – and this is a very worthy sentiment. But in Leslie's eyes something very different was going on: '. . . they never let you read on your own – they say, ''he's no good, we'll hear him'' – they never give you a chance . . .' Certainly when Leslie said this to me as part of our taped chats I was very surprised, always having tried to help the poor readers in just the way he was complaining about! It was another startling example of our failure as teachers to see things through the eyes of the children. But the point I am trying to make here is that during these quiet reading sessions the teacher has a real opportunity to read children's literature as well. At my last school we had twenty minutes of silent reading every day: one hundred minutes a week, one thousand minutes a term, three thousand minutes (fifty hours) a year! I have to admit that, contrary to my expectations, I used to read far more children's literature at school than I now do at a college of education! In addition to providing a golden opportunity for teachers to keep up with the world of children's books, such sessions also created a very positive atmosphere in the classroom. Teacher reading gave status to the activity in the children's eyes – it must be worth while if I was so engrossed in it. When I opened my book I found that the children settled much more easily to their books and a lovely 'reading calm' enveloped the room.

A teacher who knows about and is enthusiastic about children's books can then pass on this enthusiasm, even to children who find it difficult. With this in mind we can turn to other aspects of the reading session which can encourage these children to behave like 'real' readers. Apart from the actual reading together the teacher can engage in talk with the child about the book being read. Some of this will, hopefully, be the sharing of enthusiasm for particular qualities of the book, in much the same way that two people who have seen the same film or play will discuss their reactions:

'Wasn't it good!'
'What about the bit where . . .'
'I didn't half laugh when . . .'
'I didn't like the ending.'

Such sharing of a common experience is something that people indulge in with great enthusiasm and applies equally to the reading of books. With the poor reader it also draws attention to the real point of reading and away from a concern with surface features. However, the reading of a story or novel is also a chance to involve children in a consideration of aspects both of the reading process and of the work itself. Before a reader begins the first chapter of a novel, certain expectations will have been aroused as to the content and his enjoyment of it. As he embarks on his reading he will have at the back of his mind certain preconceived notions concerning what the novel will be about. Then during the reading, aspects of the reading process (as demonstrated by Sally) will determine the reader's response and can be profitably and enjoyably discussed. Finally when the novel is finished the reader can look back at aspects of it which may now be clearer or at parts which were particularly enjoyed. Such an approach to a reading session will now be discussed.

1 'What's the book going to be about?'

a. *Title*

Titles of novels can be fascinating. A title may be informative, it may summarize, it may be ironic, it may be a quotation from another literary work, it may be the name of a central character, it may indicate the novel's theme, it may be (and frequently is) a puzzle. Readers, whether adult or child, are bound to wonder about what the title might mean as they embark on the reading. And as they read, the title will be at the back of their minds constantly affecting the reading. A list of titles of popular children's novels makes the point: *The Way to Sattin Shore* (Philippa Pearce), *The Green Book* (Jill Paton-Walsh), *The Stone Book* (Alan Garner), *The Snow Spider* (Jenny Nimmo), *The Turbulent Term of Tyke Tyler* (Gene Kemp), *The BFG* (Roald Dahl). Readers who know these works will know exactly what the titles mean, but they will mean little when the books are opened for the first time. In some cases the meaning will become clear very early in the story (e.g. *The BFG*) while in others we have to wait almost until the closing lines to understand why the author chose a particular title (e.g. *The Stone Book* and *The Green Book*). Another work can be used to further illustrate the expectations and curiosities fed by titles: *Carrie's War* by Nina Bawden. In this case who is Carrie? Is he or she a soldier; involved in fighting a war; living through a war; the cause of a war; or is it that he or she is simply fighting some sort of battle? Is it gang warfare? And so on. And while early on we realize that we are reading about the war experiences of a girl and her brother who are evacuated to Wales, at what point (if ever) do we begin to connect the title with the 'war' Carrie fights with Mr Griffiths?

I have found that the expectations set up by titles can be fruitful grounds for discussion with children who are sharing books with me. Sometimes a decision has to be made concerning whether or not a particular title requires explanation, not in order to explain its significance in terms of the novel before it has been read but because the child reader may not appreciate the meaning of the title at all. I remember reading the short story 'Spoil the Child' by Howard Fast to some 12-year-olds and asking if this title meant anything to them. When it appeared not to do so, I asked who knew the expression 'spare the rod and spoil the child' and again no-one did. Having focused on it, however, it provided them with a way into an appreciation of the story. This session drew my attention to the way in which many children simply accept the titles of novels, never even reaching the stage of being puzzled by them. Poor readers often exemplify this passive acceptance of what is offered to them as reading material. It surely must be important that they begin to actively interact with the different features of the books they read. There are adult novels which, while they can be read and appreciated without the titles being understood, take on a new dimension when the derivation of the titles is realized. Steinbeck's *The Grapes of Wrath* is a good example, for one needs to know that it is a phrase from The Battle Hymn of the Republic in order to appreciate why it was chosen. Another is Hemingway's *For Whom the Bell Tolls*, coming as it does from a sermon by John Donne. Titles are then important aspects of the reading process and children who have failed with reading should come to see them as such.

b.   *Cover*

In recent years it has become commonplace for both hardback and paperback editions of children's novels to be illustrated in some way. Of course, these designs are chosen by publishers, not authors, but like titles they can certainly affect the way a reader reads. Sally, whose reading of *Tom's Midnight Garden* formed the basis of Chapter 4, stated after only having read the first chapter that she thought Tom would meet a girl in old-fashioned clothes. When asked for the reason for this prediction she said: 'Well, it shows him with a girl on the cover.'

Just as the title can offer clues to the theme or the action of a novel, so too can the cover illustration. In addition, they can both offer a way into a deeper appreciation of the work. A good example is the Puffin edition of Betsy Byars' *The Night Swimmers,* showing as it does the figure of a girl under water, perhaps drowning. The main character in the story does indeed turn out to be a girl and the reader awaits the scene in which she must get into difficulties in the water. But no such scene occurs. As an adult reader I had become aware, by the end, of the cover being an illustration of the way in which Retta is indeed 'drowning' as she tries to act as a mother to her brothers (their real mother having been killed in a plane crash). I was reminded of Stevie Smith's poem 'Not Waving but Drowning'. Because, before we read the novel, we had discussed the cover and the expectations it set up, when we finished I was able to lead the children into an appreciation of the reason for it.

However, there are problems with covers which can result in them interfering with the way in which we read. Firstly there is the way in which readers form images as they read (see Chapter 4). These pictures in the mind are very personal, readers mixing people and scenes from their own lives with the descriptions in the text. If a school is the setting for a story I tend to imagine aspects of schools I have known which seem to fit what is being described. Illustrations can interfere with this process. I am left with the picture on the cover and prevented from forming my own. Secondly cover illustrations can give away important developments in the story before the reader has reached them. A major aspect of the reading process is the way we predict our way through what we read, and a major part of the writer's task is to lead us through the plot. A good example is the cover of the Puffin edition of *Walkabout* by James Vance Marshall which shows two school children and an aborigine in the desert. The first part of the novel describes the two children struggling to survive after a plane crash in the Australian outback. The reader is forced to wonder whether and how they will survive. The shock of their meeting with the aborigine boy is cleverly sprung upon us. However, the cover has already shown the three of them together. All of the author's skill in building up the tension is wasted.

Discussion of the part played by the cover in affecting the way we read a work of fiction can and should go on in reading sessions. As a follow-up activity the designing of alternative covers can be a fascinating exercise. In addition children can be asked to choose key scenes from the book and illustrate them in some way. Only a reader who has fully understood what he has read will be able to do this. And again attention is focused on the 'meaning' of the work and away from 'getting the words right.'

c.   Publisher's blurb

The blurb on the cover or inside the front of novels can be a strong determining factor in whether the book is chosen to be read. When asked why they chose a particular book children will often reply, 'Well it sounded good.' Children with reading difficulties, in my experience, do not make much use of this 'guide', the main reason being that they rarely get the chance to choose books for themselves! All too often it is the teacher's choice that they read because it is thought to be of the right level of 'difficulty' for them. When given the chance the blurb is just another part of the reading which surrounds them and which they feel they will be unable to read. In order to help we need to read the blurb with the child and talk about it so that he is again able to function as a 'real reader'. One note of warning though follows from what was said about cover illustrations above. The publisher's blurb really can give away an awful lot of what is to be read. *Walkabout* has already been used as an example with regard to its cover, and the blurb on the back cover gives away even more:

> Mary and her young brother Peter are the only survivors of an air crash in the middle of the Australian desert. They are facing death from exhaustion and starvation when they meet an Aboriginal boy who helps them to survive, and guides them on their long journey; and then, because of a tragic misunderstanding, Mary causes his death. An unusual and haunting book which will appeal to all thoughtful readers.

So before a reader begins this novel, he knows without a shadow of a doubt that the aborigine boy is going to die. The tension leading up to this occurrence, so movingly conveyed by the author, is all to no avail. The reader already knows the outcome.

I tested this particular edition of the novel with a class of 13-year-olds, reading the story aloud while the children either listened or followed in their own copies. A third of the way through, the class was divided into groups and asked to predict what they thought would happen. Two of the groups had not read the blurb, it having been taped over on their copies, while the other groups had done so. The group predictions clearly showed the importance of the blurb. All the groups who had read it thought (actually of course they knew!) that the aborigine was going to die. Generally they hoped that he would first lead the children to safety (a boy in one group also wrote that he hoped the aborigine would not die even though he knew he would!). However, the two groups who had no knowledge of what was to happen produced different predictions. Both thought (and hoped) that the aborigine would lead the children to Adelaide. One group then thought that he would return to his tribe while the other group hoped he would be adopted by the children's family and live with them. Neither group mentioned the possibility of his dying.

Examples similar to this one can be found throughout the entire range of published novels and are bound to have an effect on the way these novels are read. Talking about this with children can be a fascinating exercise – indeed a number of the class described above vowed never to read the blurb on a novel again!

The aspects of novels described above (the title, cover illustration and publisher's blurb) should nonetheless become a natural starting point for a reading session in which a new book is begun. The children we work with should not only come to see them as useful guides as to whether they will enjoy the book but also appreciate how they will affect their response. The latter point means that these features can be referred to throughout the reading at moments when connections are made between them and what is being read. As part of the conversation which should precede the starting of a new book I also like to refer to two other features, the date of the publication and the author. Children are fascinated to discover how old the novel is that they are reading, but they need to be shown where to look! Any information about the author is also of interest: do we know how old he/she is or where they live? Is there a photograph of them? Articles in the books and journals listed in the appendix often contain such information as well as fascinating insights into the writing of novels. For example Nina Bawden's article 'A Dead Pig and My Father' in *Writers, Critics and Children* shows how she came to write *The Peppermint Pig*. I remember hearing Gene Kemp say that *The Turbulent Term of Tyke Tyler* was a story about 'love', which initially surprised me but which led to an excellent discussion of it with some 11-year-olds.

2   What kinds of things happen to us when we read?

a.   *Reminders*

If, as I hope I have demonstrated above, readers bring themselves to the reading of stories and novels, interacting with what the author writes, then we ought to allow the children we work with to explore this whole area. It may sound complex but in reality it is very simple and hinges on one question: 'Does anything in the story remind you of things in your life?'

This could refer to the plot (have you ever felt frightened/sad/excited/ depressed like this!), the characters (do you know anyone like this!), or the setting (does this place remind you of somewhere you know!). Of course, I am not suggesting that we batter children with such questions; rather that through their use as part of sensitive teaching children come to a realization of what reading novels is all about. Some of our connections will be extremely private and not open to discussion, but the exploration of many really can develop children's ability to respond to the stories they read.

b. Pictures in the mind

The forming of mental images during reading has already been discussed in Chapter 4. Remember Sally: 'No, I see a picture. I'm looking at the whole room, with Tom over in one corner and the grandfather clock by him ...'

The exploring of these images can be extremely fascinating and easily initiated by asking: 'Close your eyes, think of the story. What do you see?'

While the responses hinge on what the author has written, they also include the sorts of personal connections mentioned above: reminders of places visited, people known, and so on. The short story 'Spoil the Child' mentioned earlier provoked a lot of images from western films. Different readers will describe different images at different points in a story and I have found that these differences can lead to fascinating discussion.

c. Who/where were you?

The ways in which readers feel for different characters and the viewpoints from which they 'watch' different scenes were illustrated in Chapter 4. Sally demonstrated dramatically the strength of her involvement with Susan in *The Lion, the Witch and the Wardrobe:* 'I was Susan and I would never believe Lucy when she told me that she'd gone into another world, and I was there and I was telling her it wasn't true!'

She also described herself as a spectator of the events in *Tom's Midnight Garden:* 'With Tom I'm looking through something being able to see him . . . and I'm watching Hattie in the scenes.'

It was very evident when talking to Sally that she much preferred books in which she really could 'identify' with one of the characters. Michelle and Helen were two 10-year-olds who read Nina Bawden's *The Peppermint Pig,* and they expressed similar feelings. Michelle explained: 'In this book I'm Poll, but in *Murder on the Orient Express* I was no-one. I was just looking at it really.' She seemed to have moments when she actually imagined herself to be Poll but these all occurred in the first half of the novel. Once Poll's behaviour began to deteriorate she distanced herself from her. The turning point was Poll's fight with Noah, for although Michelle believed Poll should have 'stuck up' for her brother, Theo, she definitely should not have got involved in a fight for him. After this incident Michelle summed up her feelings as, 'I think I'm looking at her now.' When Helen began *The Peppermint Pig*, her sympathies were quickly drawn towards Poll and she seemed to find no difficulty imagining herself to be in Poll's place:

Helen   You feel as though you're there and watching what's happening. You're in there with them. I imagine I'm one of them. I'm Poll.

Q   Where are you in the scene?

H   Underneath the table with her.

Q   You're with her?

H   Well I'm Poll.

Like Michelle, Helen's response altered with Poll's behaviour and, when she had read the episode in which Poll is very rude to her mother and goes to Annie's house (which her mother had forbidden her to do), Helen's viewpoint changed: 'Well, I think Poll has changed. I think she thinks more of herself than she did. I'm not with her as much as I was. I'm looking at her now – watching her. The scene where she's cheeky – I wish I wasn't there watching it'.

Helen's last comment dramatically indicates the strength of her involvement in the novel. It would perhaps be true to say that the greater the involvement the less the reader stands back to consciously consider as he reads. Whether a reader gets involved at all will depend on the subjective factors described earlier. No two readers will read the same novel in the same way. The exploration of this aspect of reading through a simple question such as 'Where were you in that scene?' can, again, be fascinating.

d. Predicting

Prediction is a process we all engage in while reading fiction, both in the sense of wondering what will happen next and in the way we try and organize what is happening into a coherent whole. We expect some sort of pattern and wonder how everything will fall into place at the end. Sally, in Chapter 4, predicted her way through *Tom's Midnight Garden* and even though most of her predictions turned out to be wrong, this did not appear to lessen her enjoyment of the novel. This process is not, however, a cold, objective judgement based on the evidence presented by the text. As we bring so much of ourselves to any reading, and enter into the lives of the characters we are reading about, so we will hope and fear for them. We can then explore this aspect of reading by asking three questions:

'What do you think will happen?'
'What do you hope will happen?'
'What do you want to happen?'

All three will rely heavily on an understanding and appreciation of what is being read, but will also allow children to express their active involvement with it.

e.   *Puzzled?*

The ability of a reader to understand what is happening in a novel is obviously necessary for any 'significance' to be possible, but exactly how much understanding is required seems to be debatable.

Pleasure and involvement can (and often do) precede full understanding, and could I ever say that I have fully understood any novel I have read? The process of predicting is complemented by that of looking back on what has happened. How one predicts will depend on how one has responded to what has happened in the novel so far.

Two different aspects of understanding are important and are well illustrated from the work done with a class of 12-year-olds, referred to earlier, who read Howard Fast's short story 'Spoil the Child'. Having read the first couple of pages, the class were given the opportunity to ask questions and it became apparent that their awareness of the facts concerning settlers in their covered wagons trying to make lives on the hostile plains of North America varied greatly. Some children had very little idea where the family were or why. This, then, is the first level of understanding and poses the question of how much information should be given by the teacher to 'aid' the reading. As adults what do we need to know of Charles Dickens' England or Hardy's Wessex before we can really appreciate their work? What seems to be required of teachers reading novels with children is the ability to provide necessary background information without letting this interfere with the story being read. The main reason for enjoying Nina Bawden's *Carrie's War* and Michelle Magorian's *Goodnight Mr Tom* is the involvement with the characters. Both require some knowledge of the evacuation of children during the Second World War, but learning about this is not the major consideration.

The second level of understanding is illustrated in 'Spoil the Child' by the reaction of the children to mother's 'illness'. At different points in the reading they were asked to write down privately anything they wished about mother. A wide range of awareness was apparent. Some children had suspected early on that mother was pregnant while to others the birth, near the end, came as a great surprise. If our aim is to develop the individual response of children to their reading, then the danger of the teacher giving the game away early should be obvious. If the teacher has read the book before, she will pick up clues to future developments and may well draw the attention of the child reader to them before they really signify anything on a first reading. Even if the teacher is reading the book for the first time with the child, as an experienced reader she will pick up what is going on at a faster rate. It seems to me to be necessary to exercise great caution when deciding to draw the attention of children to particular developments. Sometimes it may well be necessary, but at others it would be far better to let the children pick up what is happening at their own pace and in their own way. It would have been a shame to have 'explained' to all of the children reading 'Spoil the Child' at the same time that mother was expecting a child.

3. 'We've finished!

Two different points can be made about reading sessions in which books are finished.

a. *Sharing the excitement*

Most importantly, teacher and child should simply sit back, relax and share their reactions to what has been read in the same way that people do after sharing any experience together; seeing a film or play perhaps, listening to some music or wandering around an art exhibition. This surely is what we all want to do at such times. (As teachers we need to remember this when we feel that seemingly natural teacherly behaviour coming on of bombarding children with questions in order to check on comprehension!) We want initially to chat in clichés: 'Wasn't that tremendous/awful/fantastic . . .' 'I really did enjoy that,' 'That was so funny', etc. Then reference will be made to particular aspects: a scene, movement or painting. Why these had such an effect will be expressed and either agreed with or not. And so the conversation will go on in an easy, non-threatening way – people drawn together in a very special relationship by having shared an artistic experience. If we are to use literature with children who have difficulty reading (or those who are reluctant readers) then this chatting about books shared must be our goal. Our role as teachers must be to bring such children to an awareness of its worth.

b. *Looking back*

This sort of sharing of the excitement of books read allows us to draw the child's attention again to those features of the book and the reading process described above. Again it must be stressed that this should be done in a very 'informal' way as part of a 'natural' conversation. We do not want children (especially those who have experienced failure with reading) to see the sessions as being concerned with questions and answers. When I carried out the work with the fluent readers which has been referred to throughout the book I found I had to spend a lot of time initially making them realize that they were not about to do a 'comprehension exercise'. In saying that I wanted them to read a novel over a few weeks and then talk to me about it, their expectations seemed to be that I would ask questions of the sort they were used to from English course books. Previously I had objected to such work because I felt it reduced literature to a boring exercise, but I now realized that in fact it was absolutely irrelevant to the reading of novels. We just do not read stories in the way implied by comprehension questions! Once the children realized that it was their responses to the books which I was interested in, they began to talk more freely, making the comments which I have quoted.

I always found it interesting then to refer back to the title and cover illustration and discuss their meaning and suitability. The producing of alternative covers has already been mentioned and the thinking up of alternative titles can be equally rewarding. In the same way the writing of a new publisher's blurb which will attract readers without giving away too much can be a joint exercise between teacher and child. If the child has severe problems with writing, the teacher can act as scribe while the child composes. Exactly how all the predictions turned out can be explored, and this leads to a consideration of how 'satisfying' is the author's ending. Similarly, by closing one's eyes and thinking of the book, the pictures in the mind can be discussed. This often leads on to what can be the most rewarding of the areas, the linking of the book with anything from the readers' own lives: people and places known, experiences, feelings.

It is not being suggested that the above areas be worked through religiously with every book shared. Rather they seem to me to be aspects of the reading process which occur naturally when fluent readers read novels and stories. We do not need to develop them in children who have learnt to read easily and 'unconsciously' and who are now avidly reading as many books as they can, because they are a part of the whole process. But children who have failed with reading do not appreciate what it is that fluent readers do. As Leslie shows in Chapter 1, reading becomes a search for a way to cope with the surface features of letters, sounds, blends and words. Such children need to have their attention drawn away from this search and towards the ideas, feelings, images and connections with our own lives that makes reading novels such a powerful experience. The paired reading variation described in the last chapter enables us to do this – to really share novels and stories with the strugglers and open the door onto the world of 'real' reading.

Poetry

In the introduction I stated that books concerned with children who had reading difficulties did not have chapters about responding to novels and stories. Rather a skills-based approach is advocated which is concerned with improving the child's ability on the surface features. This book is an attempt to draw the attention of teachers working with such children to aspects of the reading process and reader-response which they may well miss but which could be a way into reading for many children. With regard to poetry the situation is even more depressing for I have rarely seen evidence of its use with children who require help with their reading. Yet its power is surely indisputable. In poems, language is used at its most concentrated to reflect on experience. Perhaps this is the source of the problem, for if our aim is to provide reading matter in which the language has been purposely 'simplified', poetry could not be included.

Earlier in the book I have argued against this view of the sort of reading material we should present to children and there is no point repeating the argument here. In addition, the need to be aware of the ways in which readers bring so much of themselves to reading applies equally to poetry. Quite why I find a particular poem moving will be due as much to the sort of person I am as to the words on the page. Last year I read Douglas Dunn's collection *Elegies* and for me this was an extremely emotional experience. Talking to friends, I know that I was not alone in being affected so much by these poems. But I am sure that there must be other people for whom they meant very little. The point is, though, that I have experienced the power of poetry. I know what words on a page can do. This seems to me to be the only qualification required by anyone wanting to use poetry with children (with the addition of a willingness to search out poems suitable for sharing with them). I do not intend to argue the case for poetry in any detail; many teachers reading this will share with me a belief in its power and will therefore not need convincing. Teachers of reading who are unconvinced need perhaps to read some.

The paired reading described in the last chapter works as well for poetry as for stories and novels, with the added bonus that popular poems can be re-read over and over; and the approach I would advocate as part of the reading programme is very simple. To begin with, until poetry has become established, the teacher needs to choose the poems to be read (as time passes the children can be given the chance to choose) and, for the sort of children we are concerned with in this book, they need to have an 'instant' appeal. Luckily there are a number of poets writing for children today whose work is eminently suitable in this respect and a list appears in the appendix. There really are a great number of anthologies on the market at the present time, generally illustrated beautifully, which will provide more than enough choice for years of shared reading sessions. I have started with 10- and 11-year-olds using Michael Rosen's poems, and the collection *Let's Get Out Of Here* has never failed. Not only are these superb for paired reading in terms of both the language and their length (some are three or four pages long) but they are immediately popular. Many of them concern Eddie, a 2-year-old boy, and a favourite starting point has been 'Eddie And The Nappy':

> Eddie hates having his nappy done
> So I say all cheery,
> 'Time for your nappy Eddie,'
> and he says, all sad,
> 'No nappee.'
> And I say,
> 'Yes nappy.'
> So I have to run after him going,
> 'Nappy nappy nappy nappy ...'

> And he's got these little fat rubbery legs
> that go round like wheels;
> so away he runs
> with a wicked grin on his face
> screaming,
> 'Woooo woooo woooo.'

So I go running after him
shouting,
'Nappy nappy nappy,
I'll get you I'll get you …'
Until I catch him.
Then I lift him up.
lay him over my knees
to get his nappy off.

While I'm doing the pins
he gargles,
'Geeereegreegeereegree,'
waving his podgy little legs in the air.
He thinks,
great. Time to kick Dad's chin.
And smack smack smack
on my chin.

When I've cleaned him up
it's time for the cream.
You have to put cream on a baby's bum
or they get nappy rash.
But we leave the jar of cream
on the window-sill
where it gets all cold.
So I go,
'Time for the cream Eddie.'
And he goes,
'No cream.
So I say
'Yeah, cream.'
And I blob it on
and he goes, 'Oooh.'
You imagine what that would feel like.
A great blob of cold cream.
It would be like
having an ice-lolly down your pants.

So then I put the nappy on
and away he goes on those little rubbery legs
going
'Woooo woooo woooo.'

I have read this poem successfully (in that a lot of laughing goes on at different parts) to infant children, top juniors and 20-year-old student teachers! Children with reading difficulties request it and get tremendous satisfaction from being able to read it themselves. Other poems in the collection are equally amusing but there are also more serious ones. 'Going through the old photos', for instance, is very sad and yet equally accessible to children.

One reason for the success of these poems is that they are rooted in everyday experiences with which young readers can identify. Frequently they tell a story, which brings us back to the power of narrative, and in this respect a great number of suitable poems are to be found among traditional ballads. Here we find simple language, a narrative either explicitly told or hinted at and themes which are basic to all our lives. Add to this strong rhymes and rhythms and the reason for the ballads' lasting popularity becomes plain. With 12- and 13-year-olds I found the anthology *Voices 2* an excellent starting point, containing as it does many ballads (both traditional and modern) suitable for paired reading sessions. 'The Twa Corbies' with its Scottish dialect, which fascinates non-Scots, and its bleak view of love, betrayal and death is extremely powerful, the final verse being:

> Many a one for him maks mane,
> But nane shall ken whar he is gane,
> O'er his white banes when they are bare,
> The wind shall blow far evermare.

More recent industrial ballads such as 'The Gresford Disaster' are also worth using, and modern works by Charles Causley become great favourites. His 'The Ballad Of Charlotte Dymond' (in *Voices 2*) has been requested over and over again by some children who are quickly able to read it with very little help. Perhaps it is the contrast between verses such as:

> Her cheeks were made of honey,
> Her throat was made of flame,
> Where all around the razor
> Had written its red name.

and the texts of 'remedial' schemes which has something to do with this. What a mistaken view of helping children read is the producing of story books in 'simple language', all the life having been drained out of them. Language must be a living, vibrant part of reading for all children as it is in these poems. And 'The Ballad Of Charlotte Dymond' really does touch something deep inside its readers, whether they be fluent adults or struggling 12-year-olds.

The strong rhymes and rhythms of ballads are a key to a very different sort of poetry which younger children find equally exciting. The 9-year-olds I worked with loved learning off by heart nonsense verse, Leslie (from Chapter 1) beginning with:

> I had a baby brother
> His name was Tiny Tim
> I put him in the bath tub
> To teach him how to swim
> He drank up all the water
> He ate up all the soap
> He died last week
> With a bubble in his throat

The poem goes on to relate, very repetitively, how different characters (the doctor, the nurse and the lady with the alligator purse!) come into the house, pronounce the baby dead and then leave. The satisfaction Leslie and the others got from reciting this, and others similar, over and over to me and to each other, took me by surprise. But, of course, this was success, something they could do, so I should not have found it surprising. We learnt others, complete with actions, the most popular being 'There was an old woman who swallowed a fly', and performed them to other classes in the school. Always these performances were greeted with enthusiastic applause. If changing the self-image of these children is to be a key feature of our work, the satisfaction and excitement they obviously felt after these performances made them worth ten thousand worksheets.

Poetry, then, became a natural part of my work both with individual children and with groups. Sometimes whole reading sessions were taken up with it, while at other times a poem would simply be read and then left for another day. This latter strategy was designed to allow children to read a poem on a number of occasions before talking about it. I have always found it difficult to 'respond' to particular poems after a first reading (and yet this is not how poetry is approached so often in schools; and if not instant response, then something even more awful: instant comprehension questions?) needing to get acquainted with them before really sorting out what I think and feel. It is the same with music. My response to a particular record will often change after I have heard it on a number of occasions. This is the example I tend to use with children when explaining that they will read a poem on three or four occasions before we will talk about it. What one finds is that by the fourth reading (the readings spread out over a week or ten days) the children have begun to remember particular lines and verses. Language has begun to weave its magic spell. Poems become 'internalized' and the children 'make them their own', able then to talk about particular bits and their feelings towards them. Or we can all simply sit back quietly in the knowledge that we have shared something very special: something which has touched us deeply, perhaps in different ways, almost certainly for different, personal reasons, and which has made us realize again what reading is all about.

The use of real literature with children who have experienced difficulty learning to read is, in my view, seriously underestimated, and it is in the hope of drawing the attention of teachers of such children to the potential of literature that I have written this book. Much of the evidence used to support my case has come from children themselves, both fluent readers and strugglers. Perhaps we need to ask the children more often just what they make of the work we do with them. To conclude I would like to summarize the main arguments I see as crucial in the approach I have advocated.

1   Children who fail to learn to read search consciously and desperately for the key to read success. They seek clues in the work presented to them by

teachers. If such work concentrates on the learning of sounds, letters, blends, words (the surface features) then the children think that in these lies the way forward. They think that fluent readers work these out in order to read. So they concentrate their attention on them when they read. As Leslie said: 'That's what I kept doing – trying on the letters – oh, if I could get this alphabet I could read all the words. But I didn't – I couldn't read all the words.'

2 Fluent readers are not conscious of sounds, letters, blends or most of the words. They read the ideas behind these surface features. It is through their interaction with these ideas that they make sense of and respond to the text. To quote Sally: In *The Lion, the Witch and the Wardrobe* I was Susan and I would never believe Lucy when she told me she had gone into another world, and I was there and telling her it wasn't true!'

3 The paired reading variation described earlier allows children who have failed before, to read like fluent readers. They are able to concentrate on the ideas in the text and attention is diverted away from the surface features.

4 We are then able to use 'real' books (both stories and poetry) with these children: writing which really is worth interacting with; writing to which they really can respond. Here, the power of narrative is used to take the children along. Narrative is a basic human characteristic, the way in which we organize our lives. We tell stories each and every day as we recount to others or to ourselves our experiences. The power of a good story can be seen in pre-school children (see Chapter 3) and stays with us throughout our adult lives.

5 Written language has a rhythm all of its own. By paring down language in simplified reading books we lose not only this rhythm but also the richness of vocabulary so necessary for these children. In addition we lose the redundancy of language which helps us through written texts. Perhaps these simplified texts actually make learning to read more difficult.

6 Modern literary critics have drawn attention to the ways in which readers interact with texts. Many of their ideas can be explored with children as part of the sharing of books during reading sessions. This helps to bring them to an understanding of what 'real', fluent reading is all about. As Margaret Spencer has written:

> If learning to read is separated from the whole world of children's literature, how can children know what is in reading for them?

Or, as Jennifer, the 9-year-old, 'atomic bomb' described in Chapter 2, said to me at the start of our first reading session: 'Bog off! I ain't reading that babby stuff!'

Appendix

Books for teachers

Achieving Literacy by Margaret Meek (RKP 1983). Quite simply the best book on children with reading difficulties. No answers but lots of questions, based on working with a number of children over a year. 'How children learn to read well is still almost a secret'.

Dyslexia or Illiteracy by Peter Young and Colin Tyre (Open University Press 1983). A good overview of recent research, plus the paired reading variation described in this book.

Reading by Frank Smith (Cambridge, new ed. 1986). The book that altered so many teachers' views of the reading process and how best to help children. The 'Twelve ways to make learning to read difficult' remains as fresh as ever.

Picture Books for Young People: 9–13 ed. by Elain Moss (Thimble Press 1986). Many picture books are excellent for both shared and silent reading. This is a useful guide to what is on the market.

Poetry for Children ed. by Jill Bennett and Aidan Chambers (Thimble Press 1986). A very useful guide to anthologies available at present.

Teaching Literature 9–14 by M. Benton and G. Fox (Oxford 1985).

Developing Response to Fiction by Robert Protherough (Open University Press 1983). Two books which go into more depth concerning reader-response and ways of developing children as active readers.

Keeping up with the market

Reviews of children's books appear regularly in both daily and Sunday newspapers, as well as in the educational press.

Recent Children's Fiction is the product of a team of reviewers from Avon and Gloucestershire drawn from every phase of education and covers books from pre-school to upper secondary. It can be obtained from:
Iain Ball (Senior Adviser for English)
Avon House North
St James Barton
Bristol   BS99 7EB

Books For Keeps, the magazine of the School Bookshop Association appears every
two months. Excellent reviews and articles. Obtainable from:
Subscription Secretary
School Bookshop Association
1 Effingham Road
Lee
London   SE12 8NZ

Poetry

a.   Instant Appeal

Jelly Belly ed. Dennis Lee (Blackie 1983)
Dirty Beasts Roald Dahl (Cape 1983)
Spooky Riddles Marc Brown (Collins 1983)
What a Lot of Nonsense John Foster (Robert Royce 1983)
Wouldn't You Like to Know Michael Rosen (Andre Deutsch 1977)
Quick, Let's get out of here Michael Rosen (Puffin 1985)
Rabbiting on and Other Poems Kit Wright (Fontana 1978)
Laughs, Hoots and Giggles J. Rosenbloom (Sterling 1984)
Knock Knock! Who's there? J. Rosenbloom (Sterling 1984)
Doctor Knock Knocks J. Rosenbloom (Sterling 1976)
Limericks Michael Palin (Hutchinson 1985)
Don't Eat Spiders Robert Heidbreder (OUP 1985)
I Din Do Nuthin John Agard (Bodley Head 1983)
Say It again Granny John Agard (Bodley Head 1986)
Tongue Twisters John Lawrence (Hamish Hamilton 1976)

b.   Anthologies

Strictly Private Roger McGough (Puffin 1981)
Poems for Over Ten Year Olds ed. Kit Wright (Kestrel 1984)
The Walker Book of Poetry for Children ed. J. Prelutsky (Walker 1983)
The Batsford Book of Stories in Verse ed. C. Causley (Batsford 1979)
Voices, The Second Book ed. G. Summerfield (Penguin 1968)

c.   Something Special

There are books in which the text and illustration combine in such a way as to
produce powerful works. Two long poems illustrated by Charles Keeping
deserve consideration in a section of their own as 'something special'.

The Highwayman Alfred Noyes (Oxford University Press 1981)
The Lady Of Shallot Alfred Lord Tennyson (Oxford University Press)

Myths, folk tales and legends

There are many anthologies on the market, some of them beautifully illustrated. These are just a few suggestions:

Tales for the Telling: Irish Folk and Fairy Stories Edna O'Brien (Pavilion 1986)

Seasons of Splendour: Tales, Myths and Legends of India Madhur Jaffrey (Pavilion 1985)

The King in the Garden Leon Garfield and Michael Bragg (Methuen 1984)

King Nimrod's Tower Leon Garfield and Michael Bragg (Methuen 1982)

Alan Garner's Book Of British Fairy Tales (Collins 1984)

The Curse of the Ring Tudor Humphries and Michael Harrison (Oxford University Press 1987)

Irish Fairy Tales Sinead de Valera (Piccolo 1979)

Scottish Fairy Tales Grant Campbell (Piccolo 1980)

The Story Spirits Annabel Williams-Ellis (Heinemann 1981)

Bibliography

Bawden, N. (1976), 'A Dead Pig And My Father'. In G. Fox *et al* (ed,) *Writers, Critics And Children*. London, Heinemann.

Benton, M. and Fox, G. (1985), *Teaching Literature 9–14*. Oxford, Oxford University Press.

Booth, W. (1983), *The Rhetoric Of Fiction*. Chicago, University Of Chicago Press.

Clark, M. (1976), *Young Fluent Readers*. London, Heinemann.

Culler, J. (1980), 'Literary Competence'. In J.P. Tompkins (ed.) *Reader-Response Criticism*. Baltimore, John Hopkins University Press.

Donaldson, M. (1978), *Children's Minds*. London, Fontana.

Holland, N. (1980) 'Unity, Identity, Text, Self ' In J.P. Tompkins (ed.) *Reader-Response Criticism*. Baltimore, John Hopkins University Press.

Inglis, F. (1981), *The Promise of Happiness*. Cambridge, Cambridge University Press.

Iser, W. (1978), *The Act Of Reading*. Baltimore, John Hopkins University Press.

Koestler, A. (1964), *The Act Of Creation*. London, Hutchinson.

Lessor, S. (1957), *Fiction And The Unconscious*. Chicago, University Of Chicago Press.

Meek, M. (1983), *Achieving Literacy*. London, Routledge & Kegan Paul.

Meek, M. (1983), 'How Do They Know It's Worth It?' In R. Arnold (ed.) *Timely Voices*. Oxford, Oxford University Press.

Protherough, R. (1983), *Developing Response To Fiction*. Milton Keynes, Open University Press.

Rimmon-Kennan, S. (1983), *Narrative Fiction: Contemporary Poetics*. London, Methuen.

Smith, F. (1986), *Reading* (new edition). Cambridge, Cambridge University Press.

Tucker, N. (1981), *The Child And The Book*. Cambridge, Cambridge University Press.

Young, P. and Tyre, C. (1983), *Dyslexia or Illiteracy? Realizing the Right to Read*. Milton Keynes, Open University Press.

Index

ballads, 78–9
Bawden, Nina, 59
behaviour of children, 21–2
Blyton, Enid, 60
Booth, Wayne, 65

Clark, Margaret, 54
colour coding, 14
comprehension, 40, 75
concentration, 18–19
copying, 16
Culler, Jonathan, 63

Donaldson, Margaret, 46–49
dyslexia, 19–21

emotions, 13

flash cards, 14

Holland, Norman, 60

Inglis, Fred, 58
Iser, Wolfgang, 39, 42, 43, 58

Koestler, Arthur, 38

language development, 31–2
language programmes, 25
Lessor, Simon, 58
literary competence, 57, 63

Meek (Spencer), Margaret, 3, 5, 57, 81

Neale Analysis Of Reading, 2

novels
   covers, 69–70
   publisher's blurb, 70–1
   titles, 68–9

oral skills, 30–2

paired reading, 52, 55–6, 81
parents 4, 15, 47–8, 50–1, 55
phonics, 21, 51
Piaget, Jean, 60
poetry, 76–80
predicting, 41, 69–70, 73
print environment, 32, 39, 52

reader – response, 3, 35, 39–45, 57–65,
   71–2
reading
   aloud, 15, 33–4, 66–7
   gaps in text, 43
   involvement with, 43, 72–3
   paired, 52, 55, 56, 81
   pictures in the mind, 42, 72
   schemes, 34, 51, 66
   shared, 4, 35
   silent, 35, 52, 55–6, 66–7
   teaching methods, 36–7
   understanding, 73–4
Rimmon-Kenan, Shlomith, 43

Smith Frank, 3
special needs, 18
story, 26, 28, 32–5, 37, 65, 78, 81

Tucker Nicholas, 60

worksheets, 24–6, 80